Kalimpong Kids

Kalimpong Kids

The New Zealand story, in pictures

JANE McCABE

OTAGO UNIVERSITY PRESS
Te Whare Tā o Te Wānanga o Ōtākou

Published by Otago University Press
Te Whare Tā o Te Wānanga o Ōtākou
533 Castle Street
Dunedin, New Zealand
university.press@otago.ac.nz
www.otago.ac.nz/press

First published 2020

ISBN 978-1-98-859236-7

Published with the assistance of Creative New Zealand

creative nz
Arts Council of New Zealand Toi Aotearoa

Editor: Imogen Coxhead

Cover: 'Brissia girls enjoying the sunshine', Kalimpong, c. 1920. Gammie family

Printed in China by Asia Pacific Offset.

MIX
Paper from responsible sources
FSC® C136333
FSC
www.fsc.org

CONTENTS

1: Introduction

MY STORY

On 1 October 2007 I arrived in the township of Kalimpong. I had reason to believe that my grandmother, Lorna McCabe (née Peters), had spent time at a residential school there. Lorna died in 1978, having never spoken of her Indian heritage, her childhood in India, or how it was that she and her siblings arrived in Dunedin in the 1920s.

One photograph led me to uncover the Kalimpong connection. While in the final stages of planning a trip to India – a long-held desire of mine – I visited my father, who at that time was residing in the house where Lorna had lived her entire adult life, in Pine Hill in Dunedin. I asked Dad if there was anything among Lorna's possessions that might help me to look into her past while in India. He produced an envelope containing a photograph of a group of girls, labelled 'Kalimpong School'. The girls' names were written on the back: Lorna and her sister Alice were both there.

A few months later I walked up the road from the township of Kalimpong to Dr Graham's Homes, clutching the photograph. Staff there immediately confirmed that I was in the right place. Over the next two days as I delved into the archives there, I learnt more about my grandmother's early life than I ever imagined possible. The original admissions book was on display in the school museum, and there were bound volumes of the *Homes Magazine*, peppered with photographs of graduates in New Zealand. The archive held a family file for Lorna and her siblings. In it were 70 letters – all the correspondence written about or by Lorna from the time she was admitted to Dr Graham's Homes in 1906 to her departure in 1920 and beyond. There were even letters written from her little house in Pine Hill.

It was a stunning way to find out about a hidden family history, but equally amazing was the discovery that Lorna had been part of a bigger story – an organised emigration scheme. I embarked on a course of research that saw me complete a doctorate at the University of Otago in 2014, published as a book in 2017. In carrying out this research I have met hundreds of descendants of Kalimpong emigrants all over New Zealand. I have been struck by the silence that was common to our family histories, and by the role that photographs played in keeping our curiosity alive. It is a thrill to finally bring to light the compelling images I have been privileged to view in these family collections.

PREVIOUS PAGES: *View from Kalimpong of Mt Kanchenjunga in the Himalayas.*
Rev Henry Simon

Woodburn Cottage group, Kalimpong, c. 1916. The author's grandmother, Lorna Peters, stands on the right with hand on hip. Lorna's younger sister Alice is in the front row, third from right. McCabe family

THE KALIMPONG SCHEME

In February 1908 two young Anglo-Indian men stepped off a ship at Port Chalmers, gateway to Dunedin city. Leonard and Sydney Williams were met by a local farmer who escorted them to their new home at Highcliff, an exposed hillside overlooking Otago Harbour.

The Williams brothers were the first two graduates to be sent to New Zealand from St Andrew's Colonial Homes (later renamed Dr Graham's Homes), a Scottish residential school at Kalimpong in northeast India. By 1938, 130 'Kalimpong Kids' had been placed in New Zealand. Each was employed by a Presbyterian family, who provided a home and support for the transition into local society. The young men would begin as farm labourers, the young women as domestic helps. Their birth families – British and Indian – were to be left behind: New Zealand, the graduates were told, was a golden opportunity to make a new and independent life for themselves. Most would never see their parents again.

This unusual life trajectory was the result of the work of a Scottish Presbyterian missionary, the Reverend Dr John Anderson Graham. Stationed in Kalimpong, Graham made it his life's work to 'rescue' the mixed-race offspring of British tea planters and local women in neighbouring Assam and Darjeeling. Because interracial relationships were beyond the bounds of social acceptability in British India in this era, the children existed in a liminal, problematic space. Graham's scheme provided a solution for tea planters who, constrained by social norms, nevertheless desired an education and a respectable future for their children.

Until 1920, small groups from Kalimpong continued to arrive intermittently in Dunedin, chaperoned on the long journey by housemothers and quickly dispersed to families around the South Island. The scheme then shifted north to Wellington where, amid growing concerns about non-British immigration, they continued to be sent to diverse locations to ensure low visibility. By the time the scheme ended in 1938, Kalimpong emigrants had been placed with families as far south as Owaka and as far north as Kaitaia. Their descendants now live all over New Zealand.

Studio portrait of Sydney Williams, taken in Dunedin shortly after his arrival in 1908. Williams family

Studio portrait of the Rev Dr John Anderson Graham, gifted to 1911 emigrant George Langmore. Langmore family

UNCOVERING THE PAST

The story of the Kalimpong migration scheme gradually faded from public view and family memory after the final group arrived in 1938. Kalimpong people were sensitive about their background, an uncomfortable subject that involved interracial relationships, illegitimacy, institutionalisation and a strong sense of abandonment. They were reluctant to discuss it in detail, and their own children often grew up with little or no knowledge of their parent's Indian heritage and subsequent pathway to New Zealand. For these descendants, understanding their family history has entailed a journey from mystery to discovery.

Graham's scheme was different from other familial interventions of the era by virtue of the network of support set up across New Zealand. New arrivals were all placed with families known to Graham through his local contacts, who established committees in each of the main centres. Many Kalimpong people were able to keep in touch with each other and, particularly in Wellington, a community spirit developed that has persisted through subsequent generations. The children of many 'Kalimpongites', as they liked to be known, remember their Kalimpong 'aunts' and 'uncles' with fondness.

Yet even for these descendants the topic has been a sensitive and hushed one, particularly when they have made concerted efforts to find out more. Andrea Stewart's grandmother Molly Chambers arrived with a group from Kalimpong in 1915. Molly settled in Wellington and was very much a part of the community there. But Andrea's search for information about her grandmother, which began in the late 1990s, still took a number of years and two trips to India. When Molly learned that her granddaughter was researching her past, she insisted that the school she grew up in had burnt down: the search for records, she said, was futile. Andrea travelled to India anyway and visited schools in Darjeeling, to no avail. Little did she realise that just a few hours' drive away, in Kalimpong, Dr Graham's Homes was still operating and had on archive a file for every pupil – Molly included.

Andrea eventually discovered the Kalimpong connection in 1999. Along with her father Malcolm, who was on his first trip to India, she was able to view Molly's personal file in the small office of this institution in the foothills of the Himalayas. As for many descendants, reading through the application forms and correspondence that detailed the circumstances of Molly's early life was an experience she would never forget.

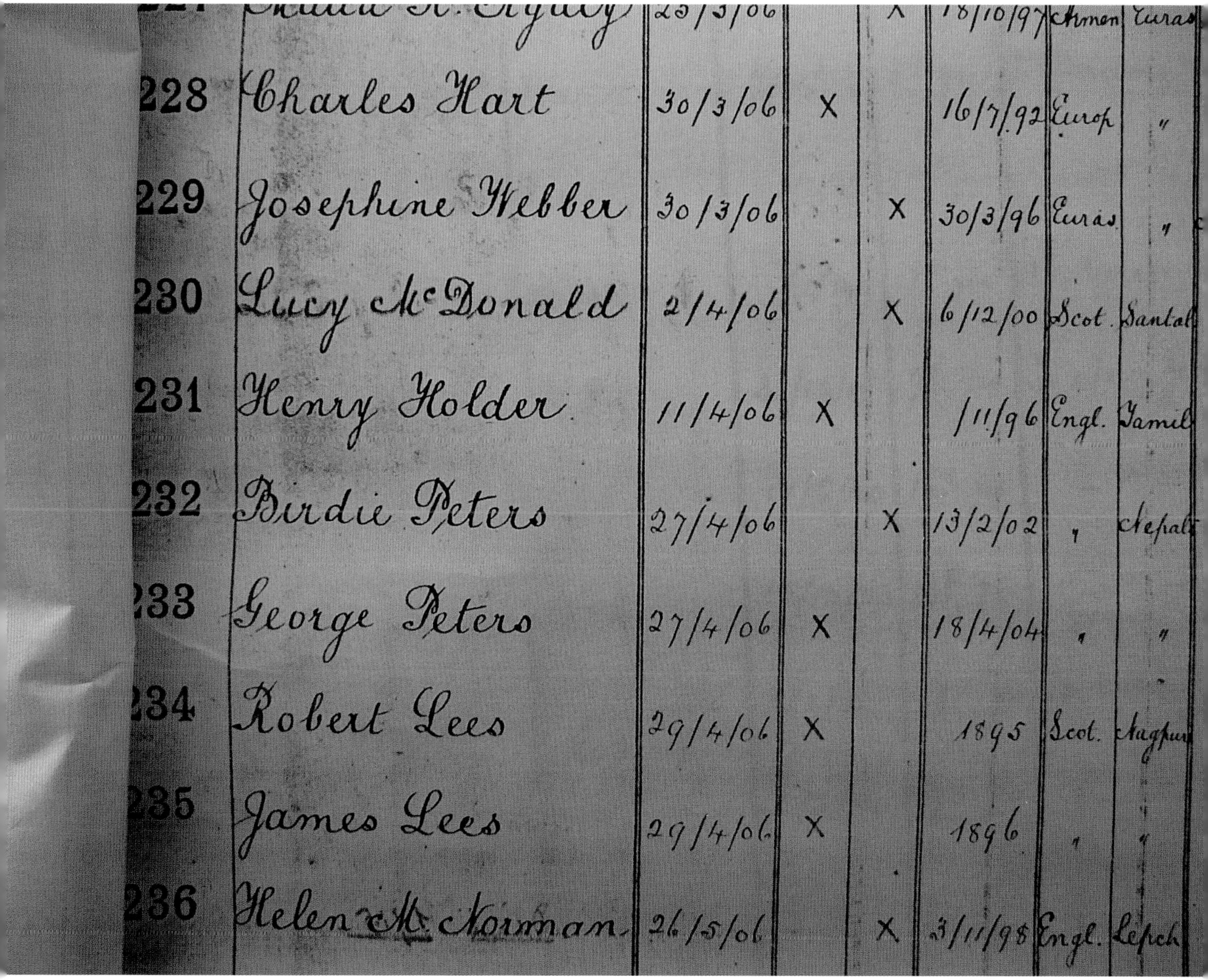

[illegible]	[illegible]	23/3/06		X	18/10/97	Armen	Euras
228	Charles Hart	30/3/06	X		16/7/92	Europ	"
229	Josephine Webber	30/3/06		X	30/3/96	Euras	"
230	Lucy McDonald	2/4/06		X	6/12/00	Scot.	Santal
231	Henry Holder	11/4/06	X		/11/96	Engl.	Tamil
232	Birdie Peters	27/4/06		X	13/2/02	"	Nepali
233	George Peters	27/4/06	X		18/4/04	"	"
234	Robert Lees	29/4/06	X		1895	Scot.	Nagpur
235	James Lees	29/4/06	X		1896	"	"
236	Helen McNorman	26/5/06		X	3/11/98	Engl.	Lepch

The original admissions book is on display in the Homes Museum at Kalimpong. This excerpt shows the entry for the author's grandmother, Lorna 'Birdie' Peters, and her brother George. Both children were admitted to the Homes in 1906 (Lorna aged four and George aged two) and stayed for fifteen years. Author

From Kalimpong to Owaka. Jean and John Mackay's ship voyage began in Calcutta on 30 April 1911, where they boarded the SS Cooyena *to Sydney. A balmy stopover in Singapore, during which this photo was taken, broke up the long voyage. They arrived in Dunedin on 18 June on the SS* Victoria *and were taken directly to their placement with families in Owaka.* *Yvonne Gale and Jon Earley*

THE PHOTOGRAPHS

Photographs have played a crucial part in recovering the stories behind the hushed Kalimpong family histories. Many descendants have inherited photographs that contain tantalising clues to a lost past. Such images enliven our engagement with family history, and provoke curiosity, discussion and imaginative speculation. They can also be a source of frustration: a constant reminder of stories unspoken and forgotten. These dynamics are a common feature of familial engagement with historical photograph albums. Historians and theorists have written extensively about the intricate processes by which photographs and memory intertwine in a kind of dance with past generations.

For Kalimpong families, photographs from India have a particular allure, evoking a sense of mystery and the exotic. The sheer beauty of the subjects or scene has sometimes been enough to ensure a photograph was kept. Most of all, they are treasured because they survived as tangible objects in a story that otherwise lies just out of reach. The fact that so many of the emigrants kept photographs from India suggests that, at some level, they were content for the next generation to discover their story in the future, beyond their time.

Yvonne Gale has vivid childhood memories of gazing at a photograph depicting her grandmother and great-uncle, Jean and John Mackay, en route from Kalimpong to Owaka. Despite Jean's silence about her heritage, the photograph would later become a permanent fixture on the mantelpiece in her Dunedin home. Like Andrea Stewart, Yvonne spent years researching her grandmother's story, at home and in England, before discovering the Kalimpong connection and eventually retrieving a copy of Jean's file. She credits her persistent research to that enticing image from her childhood.

While most families have but a few precious photographs relating to Kalimpong or tea plantations in their possession, some descendants have inherited wonderful albums – from their parents, from Kalimpong emigrants who didn't have children, or from New Zealand women who volunteered as housemothers at Dr Graham's Homes. These collections have greatly enriched the visual story told in the pages that follow. Together with photographs from Kalimpong families all over New Zealand, they reveal an extraordinary story.

2: Tea Plantations, Northeast India

PREVIOUS PAGES: *Gilbert Langmore's bungalow at Darjeeling. Gilbert's son George emigrated to New Zealand in 1911.* *Langmore family*

LEFT: *Gilbert Langmore displays the spoils of a hunting expedition.* *Langmore family*

BELOW: *Gilbert Langmore (left) hosts friends at his Darjeeling bungalow.* *Langmore family*

THE PLANTERS

British tea planters began their career in India as young men in search of opportunity. Contrary to the grand connotations of the term 'tea planter', they were employees of tea agencies rather than owners of estates. Starting out as an assistant manager, they worked their way up to the position of manager through a ten-year apprenticeship. As managers they controlled large estates of several thousand acres, with several thousand Indian workers and perhaps one or two European assistants. Tea planters were not highly paid but nevertheless enjoyed a comfortable and privileged lifestyle, though death and disease were constantly at their door.

The dangers and challenges of this existence fuelled the creation of a rich record of adventurous pursuits in northeast India. Planters wrote regular letters to family in Britain, kept diaries, and many later recounted their experiences in memoir. They took photographs of hunting exploits, sporting pastimes and social occasions. Many of these photographs have ended up in Kalimpong family collections in New Zealand – a remarkable fact in itself, and one that attests to the enduring relationship between a number of planters and their children.

In their letters home, planters occasionally bemoaned the challenging conditions of life in the 'jungle'. Few, however, wrote about the extended lonely times between social and sporting events. Frequent flooding saw them confined to the estate for months at a time; and the tea agencies had a policy of not allowing the planters to bring a British wife to the plantation until they became managers. Unbeknown to their families at home in England, many alleviated this long-term isolation by engaging in intimate relationships with women working on the plantations.

Makum Tea Estate, Margherita, Assam. Plantations were substantial estates with thousands of workers and thousands of acres planted in tea, as well as tea-processing units, worker housing, planters' bungalows, schools, hospitals and markets. Roads in and out of the plantation were strictly policed to safeguard the estate. Richard Hawkins, a 1925 emigrant, was born on this plantation. Hawkins family

ABOVE: *Francis Hawkins' bungalow, Makum Tea Estate, Margherita. In its remote setting in the far northeast of Assam, this bungalow scene portrays the reality of the planters' social isolation and guarded domestic lives. Their relationships with women workers, while an open secret on the plantation, demanded a high degree of discretion.* *Hawkins family*

LEFT: *Francis Hawkins (front row, left) poses with his polo team at Margherita, northern Assam.* *Hawkins family*

The mighty Brahmaputra River. While the introduction of railway and other technologies were integral to the development of the tea industry in northeast India, so too were local skills and knowledge – not least to harness the power of the river and the elephant. *Ruth den Boogert (née Nicholls)*

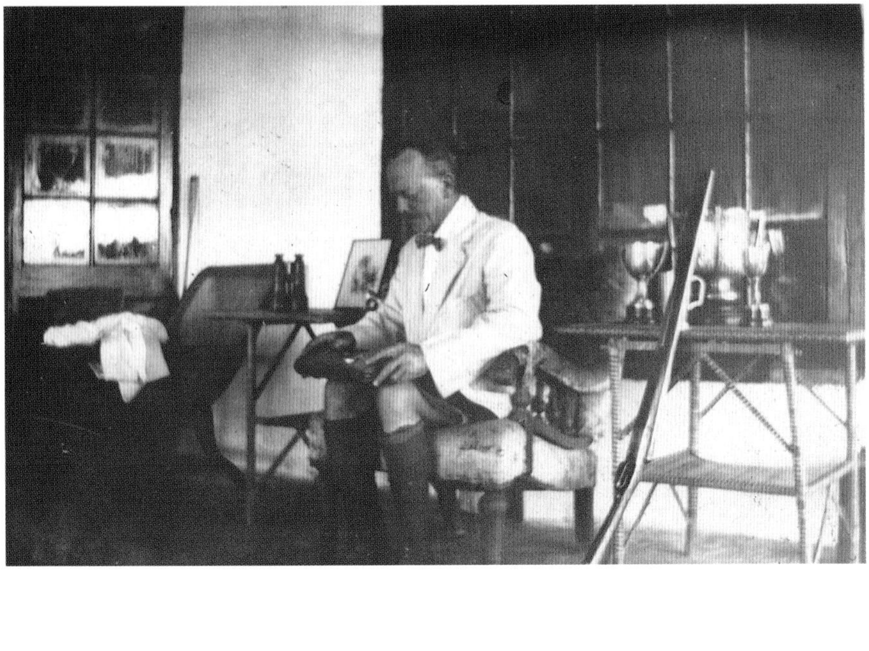

Egerton Peters, the author's great grandfather, with polo trophies and hunting paraphernalia in Cachar, Assam.
McCabe family

FRANK NICHOLLS was born in England in 1889 and left in 1912 to work on tea estates in Assam. Over his forty-year career he worked his way up to the position of manager, then superintendent, and finally tea agent.

In 1963 Frank retired to New Zealand to join his children, all of whom had been educated at the Homes in Kalimpong. There he completed a memoir of his life in tea, entitled *Assam Shikari*. There is no mention in the book of his interracial family.

Frank Nicholls, surrounded by the comforts and freedom of life as a tea planter: his furniture, clothing and tea set are markers of 'civilisation' in a cultivated garden in the midst of the jungle. He appears content – and yet, alone.

Ruth den Boogert (née Nicholls)

THE MOTHERS

The mothers of the Kalimpong Kids were part of a diverse labour force that was crucial to the establishment of the tea industry in northeast India. Alongside waves of migration from Nepal, many tea workers were recruited from famine-struck areas in India through a system of indentured labour. Locals who lived in nearby villages also took up tea work. These various communities were assigned work in the different stages of tea production, from planting to processing, and a gendered labour hierarchy and distinct social world developed on the plantation. Nepali men were employed as gatekeepers, for example, and Nepali women as housekeepers and *ayahs* (nannies). Those from famine districts were more likely to engage in manual labour: tea picking for women, and heavier pruning and processing work for men.

Many British tea planters formed relationships with women from this workforce. In contrast to their tales of adventurous pursuits and social activities, however, few left any written or visual record of these liaisons and the children that resulted. The files at Dr Graham's Homes confirm the mothers of Kalimpong Kids were of diverse origin: Lepcha, Nepali, Bengali, Assamese, Santhal, Khasi. Their names were seldom recorded. This erasure has had a profound impact on Kalimpong descendants' capacity to imagine, let alone trace, their maternal ancestry. As to what became of the women after the planters left India or died, for the majority we will never know.

The only image of one of these mothers to have surfaced thus far is that of Norah, a Khasi woman, who was the mother of 1940s emigrant Isabella Gammie (née Leith). This remnant of Norah's life is but a tiny corner, about two centimetres square, which has been cut from a photograph. Norah's granddaughter, Anne Beckett (née Gammie), had the image enlarged and it hangs in an impressive frame in her living room. The intensity of Norah's gaze befits her role in recovering the Kalimpong story. It is as if she has anticipated descendants' future queries and frustrations. We can see her, but her story – even the story of this image – is lost. Who else was pictured? Who cut Norah out, and why?

Norah, the mother of 1940s emigrant Isabella Gammie (née Leith). Gammie family

HIDDEN FAMILIES

From anecdotal evidence and third-person accounts, we know that it was common for a planter to cross the boundary of intimacy with a woman from the plantation or nearby: their housekeeper, a tea picker, or perhaps through an arrangement with a family in a local village. Because of the planters' desire to hide these relationships from the outside world, little is known about the daily lives of interracial tea plantation families.

While it was impossible for these relationships to be formalised in the social climate of the time, many were loving, long-term arrangements that produced a number of children. It was into these protected situations that John Graham stumbled in the course of his visits to tea planters in the 1890s. As he recorded in his later writing, although a planter could disguise a relationship by referring to the woman as his servant, the children with their lighter skin gave the situation away. Some planters would usher their children into the back of their bungalow and pretend nothing was amiss, but others spoke openly with Graham about their plight. When a child was young it was possible to carry on discreetly, but a shadow hung over this relatively carefree period of infancy and toddlerhood as decisions about the child's future loomed.

Valuable for their rarity, then, are photographs that depict the interior of bungalows in which these children lived, which allow us to imagine domestic life of the time. Passed down from the Langmore and Dinning families, the images impart a sense of the hybrid living spaces created by the planters, in which they blended objects and styles from Britain with local items and trophies of life in Assam. The precious photographs of Maggie and Annie Dinning speak to their father's affection for his daughters. With their constant demands for attention and interruptions to daily routines, the children must have enlivened bungalow life enormously.

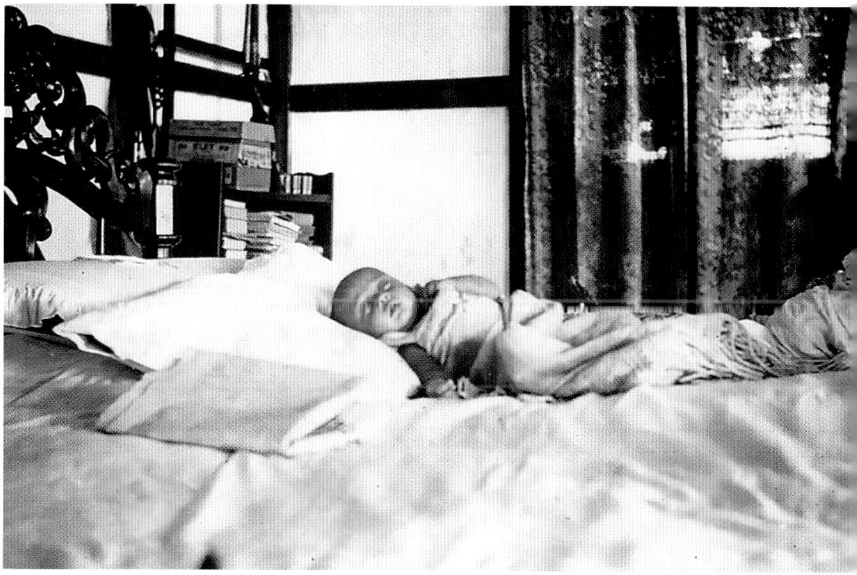

Sisters Margaret (Maggie) Dinning (above) and Annie Dinning (right). Mary Milne

RIGHT: *The interior of Gilbert Langmore's bungalow.* Langmore family

GROWING UP ON THE PLANTATION

OPPOSITE: *Frank Nicholls' children, June, Sidney, Norah and Ruth, experiencing the privileged side of a plantation upbringing alongside immersion in local life.*

BOTTOM RIGHT: *Norah and June at Kalimpong.*

Ruth den Boogert (née Nicholls)

Tea planters' children enjoyed privileged status on the large estates that their fathers managed. Indeed, they had the best of both worlds: spending adventurous days roaming around the plantation and the surrounding forest, interacting with their maternal family in the local language, and in the evenings returning to the comfortable life of a British bungalow. They were attended by servants, and were well clothed, well fed and entertained. Cared for by an *ayah*, they had a close companion by day and a steady presence to comfort them if they woke in the night.

Most British parents in India feared their children would pick up detrimental habits if allowed to mix too freely with local peoples, and routinely sent their offspring home to England for schooling. But for a tea planter with mixed-race children, this would require a public admission of his illicit relationship, and his extended British family was unlikely to accept them. After Graham opened his institution in 1900, many planters took this unique opportunity to provide for their children's future. The carefree and privileged existence the youngsters were accustomed to came to an abrupt end when they were sent to the Homes in Kalimpong, usually at the age of four or five years. Any plantation memories they may have laid down by this time faded quickly, usurped by the trauma of separation and a colossal shift in their daily routine.

Much of what we know about the experience of growing up on a plantation comes from the memories of those who were somewhat older when they were sent to Kalimpong, and those who went home from school for holidays – which was highly unusual. Ruth Nicholls speaks with great fondness of her early days on the plantation and her visits in the holidays. She enjoyed many pastimes that attest to the cultural hybridity of daily life: sitting quietly as her father listened to the BBC; enjoying the affectionate attention of her *ayah* and other household staff; moving freely around the grounds of the plantation; and playing with her sisters – tennis, or dressing up as princesses of the British royal family.

3: Dr Graham's Homes, Kalimpong

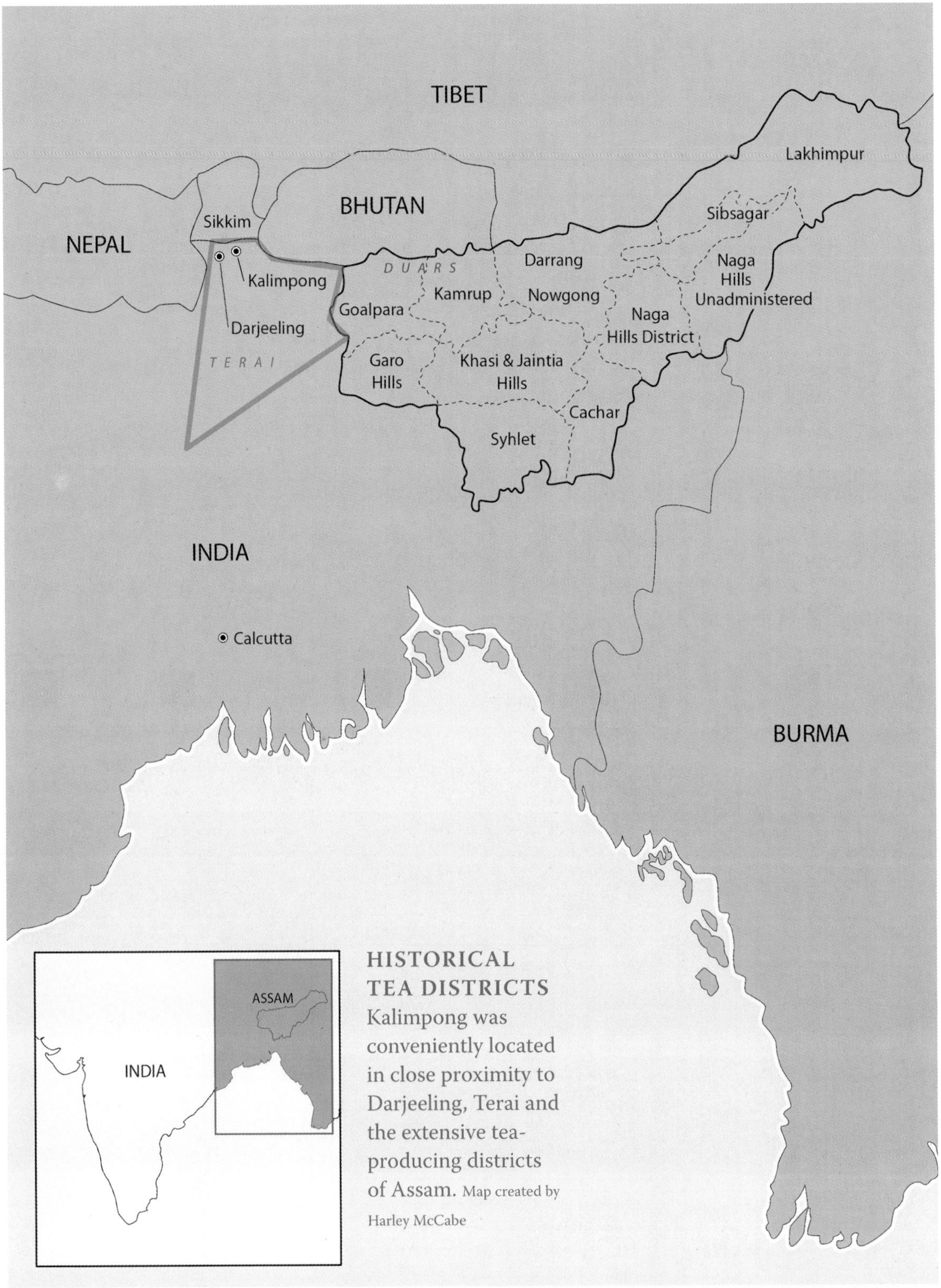

HISTORICAL TEA DISTRICTS Kalimpong was conveniently located in close proximity to Darjeeling, Terai and the extensive tea-producing districts of Assam. Map created by Harley McCabe

KALIMPONG

PREVIOUS PAGES:
An isolated setting: the Homes school buildings are centre front, with children's cottages dotted around the hillside and the township of Kalimpong in the background. Referred to locally as 'Little Scotland', the institution was typical of the bounded, protected worlds that the British tried to create within India.
Langmore family

One aspect of growing up in Kalimpong that almost all emigrants spoke of was the magnificent setting of Dr Graham's Homes in the shadow of Mt Kanchenjunga. The view of this mighty peak, the third highest mountain in the world, is made even more memorable by its rare visibility through the evocative mists that regularly shroud the town and its surrounds.

Kalimpong sits at 1250 metres in the foothills of the Himalayas, in a narrow tract of India that is bordered by four countries: Nepal, Sikkim, Bhutan and Tibet. Initially it was a tiny village, until the British established the town as a place of respite from the heat of the Indian plains – a 'hill station' comprising schools and churches, hospitals and hotels. This colonial past is evident today, and the town continues to be promoted as a place of retreat, its reputation enhanced by orchid, rhododendron and cactus nurseries that draw tourists from around the world.

The trip to Kalimpong today is still an adventurous one. The road to the town sidles through dramatic valleys and narrow mountain passes with a steep drop to the Teesta River on one side, and is often washed away by monsoon rains. Descendants are relieved and inspired when they arrive at the serene township of crumbling colonial buildings nestled in lush vegetation.

The romantic image on pages 34–35 perfectly illustrates the wistful way that Kalimpong is recalled by many who have spent time there. In one frame we take in the mountains, the mist, vegetation, simple dwellings and the slow pace of life. Taken in neighbouring Sikkim, it is part of the collection of George Langmore, who was sent to Dunedin in 1911 and made a return visit to Kalimpong in 1927.

Misty Sikkim scene.

Langmore family

ESTABLISHING THE HOMES

The Rev Dr John Anderson Graham opened St Andrew's Colonial Homes in 1900. It was renamed Dr Graham's Homes when India gained independence from Britain in 1947, and has been colloquially known as 'the Homes' since its establishment. Just as the township of Kalimpong has become associated with a kind of serenity, so too have the Homes and its founder.

Graham dreamt up his plan, to take in tea planters' mixed-race children, while working at the Church of Scotland's Kalimpong mission in the 1890s. After touring Britain from 1895 to 1898, lecturing about his experiences in India and garnering support for his proposal of a small home for forty pupils, he returned to Kalimpong and opened the first cottage. He was soon inundated with applications. From his initial vision sprang a large institution, which by the 1920s accommodated 600 children and comprised twenty cottages, numerous school buildings and workshops, a church, bakery, swimming pool, hospital and a working farm.

Into this substantial institution Graham integrated elements of his idyllic rural upbringing in the Scottish Highlands. Kalimpong boasted a healthy and temperate climate, and the isolated setting and extensive grounds, which eventually spread over 250 hectares, manifested his belief in the remedial benefits of fresh air, self-sufficiency, physical activity and hard work. Its situation meant mixed-race children could be kept at a distance from 'injurious native influence' in more densely populated areas and on the tea plantations, and afforded a degree of discretion for the tea planter who was reluctant to reveal his secret family.

ABOVE: *The heart of the Homes, late 1920s. This photograph was widely circulated by Graham and survives in numerous descendants' collections. The substantial school buildings still stand today, as does the beautiful chapel, built as a tribute to Graham's wife Katherine after her death in 1925.* Sylvia Slater (née Brooks)

LEFT: *John Graham (standing, third from right) with his daughters Bunty (left) and Betty (right) and visiting dignitaries. This photograph is remarkably different from most images that depict the Homes: it is uncharacteristically stark in tone, and local people are visible in the background.* Judi Cassidy

Graham strolls in the grounds of the church in Kalimpong. Langmore family

'Daddy Graham,' as he was known to his pupils, with two boys dressed in their best. All children at the Homes went without shoes as a cost-saving and character-building measure. Gammie family

GRAHAM'S GRAND SCHEME

Many social reformers of this era were concerned about the mixed-race communities being produced by colonial encounters, and rescue schemes sprang up in every part of the British Empire. Children deemed at risk were separated from their Indigenous families and brought up in institutions that inculcated a disciplined work ethic and manual training, with the aim of turning them into useful imperial citizens.

Graham's scheme was built on this rhetoric of rescue, but rather than risking the children being absorbed into the Anglo-Indian community at the end of their schooling, he believed the best solution for tea planters' children was to send them out of India. In this he drew on Irish philanthropist Thomas Barnardo's model of sending British children to settler colonies. Graham targeted countries where a shortage of manual labourers existed, in the hope of convincing colonial authorities to accept young people who might otherwise be seen as undesirable migrants.

Graham's plan was to take in children at Kalimpong for a period of ten to fifteen years, during which he would provide them with a high standard of British education, practical training and a boarding school-style upbringing. Upon reaching working age, youngsters would be sent to a sympathetic family in a settler colony, who would provide a home, employment and support for their transition to a new life.

In a climate of increasing anxiety about racial mixing, Graham was determined to establish a reputation for turning out respectable young people. While it was not a strict policy, he thought it better for children to stay at the Homes rather than returning to the plantations in the holidays. Although children roamed barefoot and enjoyed nature in both locations, Graham drew a distinction between allowing youngsters to run free on the plantation and the controlled liberty of the Homes. This notion of managed freedom is apparent in the images used to promote the scheme.

MITCHELL
1831-55
STURT
1828-1845
FLINDERS
1795-1810
COOK
DAMPIER
TASMAN
MARCO POLO
COLUMBUS
1492
VASCO DA GAMA
1497-1498

Schooling at the Homes was based on the British curriculum. These rare photographs from inside the school show well-equipped geography (opposite) and science classrooms (above). Judi Cassidy

Participating in sports was another means of producing robust and healthy children, and of encouraging cottage pride and competition. Gammie family

LIFE IN THE COTTAGES

Living in one cottage at the Homes for the majority of one's childhood left an impression on all who resided there. As in any British boarding school upbringing, the Kalimpong Kids moved through the phases of growing up with a cohort of girls or boys, some of whom would remain lifelong friends. In future conversations they would reminisce about the housemothers who – for better or worse – cared for them year after year. Growing up was marked not only by progression through school standards, but also by moving up a hierarchy of status and duties in daily cottage life. It was a bonding experience they would never forget.

The cottages were roughcast two-storey buildings, each with a similar layout: a kitchen and dining area were located on the ground floor and a large dormitory upstairs with single beds in neat rows. The floors were wooden and furniture was sparse. Graham embarked on a busy building programme from 1900 to 1920 to keep up with the demand for places. In order to finance construction he sought sponsorship from individuals and charities, and named cottages after these sponsors. Being a 'Woodburn girl' or a 'Fraser boy' became part of an identity forged at the Homes that was communicable across time and generations. These loyalties were rekindled when new arrivals in New Zealand sought out others from their cottage that had already settled here.

In family collections, most of the photographs that depict the Homes are portraits of children and housemothers outside their cottage. These photographs were a convenient way for Graham to respond to planters' requests for images of their children, and he also used them to promote the scheme in the *Homes Magazine*, a publication issued several times a year and circulated widely in Britain, India and the settler colonies.

A group stands outside Fraser Cottage.

Judi Cassidy

'Lucia nurses and babies, 1925.' Infants and toddlers admitted to the Homes were put into Lucia King Cottage, where 'nurses' cared for them until they reached the age of five. Lucia King Cottage was also used for training older girls in childcare and domestic duties in preparation for emigration to New Zealand. *Gammie family*

Chores before school. As soon as they were admitted to one of the main cottages, children were assigned daily household chores. Sylvia Slater (née Brooks)

Alice Smith reading the paper. Aware of his pupils' prolonged isolation at the Homes, Graham encouraged them to take an active interest in world affairs. Gammie family

RIGHT: *The Kalimpong* mela. *It is not surprising that the hustle and bustle encountered on their occasional ventures beyond the school gates forged vivid memories for the Kalimpong Kids. This image makes visible the ethnic diversity in northeast India: the majority of people in the Darjeeling district (including Kalimpong) are Nepali or Tibetan. Their warm dress is a reminder of the cooler climate here, which is often contrary to people's expectations about life in India.* *Judi Cassidy*

ABOVE: *Besides visits to Kalimpong township, the children were occasionally taken out for recreational pursuits. Picnics at Rili River were a special and memorable outing.* *Gammie family*

BEYOND THE GATES

The monotony of life at the Homes was occasionally broken by outings, under the careful guidance of a chaperone, which allowed the children to experience life beyond the school boundaries, 'down the hill' in the township of Kalimpong. The route has changed little over the course of a century: today the walk from the school gates to the township is a pleasant twenty-minute amble down a narrow road lined with sparse bush and tumble-down houses. Bundles of powerlines sag overhead, people quietly peddle their wares, and dogs and donkeys roam about.

The sense of freedom at being allowed out, and the wonder of seeing beggars, priests and traders, created lingering memories that were sometimes passed on. A visit to the Kalimpong *mela* (marketplace) was one such outing. Established by Graham in 1891, the *mela* was a busy place. It attracted traders from around the district, and is still a feature of Kalimpong social life today. Robert Ochterlony, a 1912 emigrant placed on a farm in Marlborough, noted in a letter to Graham in 1914 that rural life in New Zealand was somewhat different to the Indian environment: they hunted 'not tigers, but wild sheep', and although he had enjoyed the Blenheim A&P show, in comparison to the Kalimpong market it was 'not a very big affair'.

THE REACH OF THE HOMES

The Homes began with one cottage and four pupils. Graham originally envisaged a small facility from which all graduates would be sent to the settler colonies, but the institution grew rapidly as a result of his open-door policy. He had to fundraise extensively to keep up with demand, and eventually capped the roll at 625 in the 1920s due to financial difficulties. These high student numbers, along with increasingly restrictive immigration regimes in settler colonies, meant that most children were placed in India. Only the 'best and brightest' were to be sent abroad.

Graham was aware that businesses and charities would be less willing to donate funds to a cause that could be interpreted as providing a convenient solution to a tea planter's indiscretions. Instead, promotional material of the time suggests that the Homes were primarily a destination for impoverished children rescued from city slums, whose heritage was quite different to that of the tea planters' children. They were the offspring of Anglo-Indian parents, and their European ancestor was usually a distant figure. This reflected a long history of segregation of the Anglo-Indian community in India, where rejection of mixed-race offspring by both British and Indian sides of a family was common.

Hence the student cohort at the Homes comprised children of two distinct origins: poor city children, who were often relatively light-skinned; and tea planters' children, who had privileged beginnings and a British father, but who often inherited their mothers' physical features. As a result of these distinctions, appearance became a particular focus at the Homes: it led to teasing about particular ethnic origins, and was sometimes the only source of information children had about their maternal heritage – an uncertainty that may have contributed to their later silence. Appearance would also become a factor in deciding which children were most suited to emigration.

'Homes birthday, 1916.' A celebration of the opening of the Homes, with a gathering of the whole school and visitors and a spread of special 'buns and jelabis,' still occurs annually on 24 September. Gammie family

Janet and Mary Greig, c. 1920, prior to emigration. *Judi Cassidy*

4: Emigration

MISS KENNEDY AND TWELVE OF THE EMIGRANTS.

Farewell to our New Zealanders.

A full-page article appeared in the 1912 Homes Magazine *announcing the emigration of a group to New Zealand. Mary Kennedy (centre) was a Dunedin woman who volunteered as a housemother at the Homes. She chaperoned the 1912 group on their voyage. The names of this group can be found in Appendix Two.*

National Library of Scotland

AN ORGANISED SCHEME

For tea planters, the most appealing aspect of John Graham's scheme was the permanent resettlement of their children in overseas colonies, which enabled the continued concealment of their mixed-race families. When a planter eventually retired to Britain, his extended family need be none the wiser; and the planter could rest easy in the knowledge that his children had been given an opportunity to make a new life, far from India.

New Zealand offered good prospects for gainful employment, a reputation for egalitarianism and a history of racial mixing, and Graham saw in it a strong possibility of acceptance for Anglo-Indians. A global wave of racially restrictive immigration measures enacted at the turn of the century meant Graham faced immediate challenges to realising his vision, however. The placement of groups in Australia was never possible; and although Kalimpong graduates did cross New Zealand's borders regularly from 1908, their numbers were few and they were intentionally dispersed across the country.

Because of colonial anxieties about the racial composition of populations, Graham suspected that children with lighter complexions would have a better chance of success in New Zealand. But the children of tea planters – the men who pressured him to find placements abroad for their children and provided funds for him to do so – often inherited their mothers' darker complexion. To mitigate colonial concerns about this, Graham presented the emigrants in ways that emphasised their assimilation into Anglicised modes of dress, grooming and deportment.

Despite the planters' desperate desire for discretion, Graham needed to publicise his scheme in order to garner financial and practical support. The emigration of each new 'batch' of graduates was proudly announced in the *Homes Magazine* and some were reported in New Zealand newspapers. These articles emphasised the organised nature of the scheme, noting that each group was chaperoned by housemothers and would be met by employers on arrival.

DESTINATION DUNEDIN

The first two Kalimpong emigrants, Leonard and Sydney Williams, arrived in Dunedin in 1908. Eustace Boardman and Clarence Sinclair followed in 1909. Later that year John Graham himself visited the southern city to assess the situations of the young men who were already on farms, and as chaperone for the first young woman, Clarence's sister Aileen, to be placed as a domestic help. Clarence was waiting at the port to be reunited with his sister, along with David Kennedy, a Dunedin resident no doubt eager for news of his daughter Mary, a volunteer housemother at the Homes. Such was the nature of the tight-knit, family-centred community that began to coalesce to support this scheme.

The Reverend James Ponder and his sister Mary were responsible for the early Otago placements. Two of their siblings worked at Kalimpong, so they knew Graham well. Ponder had been a Presbyterian minister in Victoria (Australia) and Fiji before heading to New Zealand, initially to the Middlemarch parish. By 1908 he was in Waitahuna, a small rural settlement south of Dunedin. These were ideal locations in which to secure farm employment for the emigrants.

The Presbyterian Church was never officially associated with the scheme but its deep involvement was made clear during Graham's 1909 visit, when he was hosted by noted members of the Dunedin Presbyterian community. Graham was impressed with the growing city and its innovative provision of support for the sick, the elderly and other less fortunate members of society. The Ponders continued to arrange employment for young men and women from Kalimpong until James's death in 1920, by which time they had facilitated the placement of sixty youngsters with Presbyterian families in Dunedin city and its surrounds.

SYDNEY WILLIAMS, ONE OF THE RABBIT CATCHERS.

ABOVE: **JAMES PONDER**. A fellow Scot, Ponder embodied the robust and practical Christian ethic that was characteristic of Graham's supporters, and which underpinned the Kalimpong scheme. Presbyterian Research Centre (Archives), Dunedin

CENTRE: **SYDNEY WILLIAMS**. Brothers Sydney and Leonard Williams were the first two Kalimpong graduates to be sent to Dunedin. They were initially placed on farms but soon took matters into their own hands, pooling their resources and chancing their fortunes as rabbiters in Central Otago. It was a precarious existence, and not at all what John Graham had in mind when he carefully placed them with Presbyterian farming families. Nevertheless, their adventurous move was reported in the 1911 *Homes Magazine* in an article entitled 'After the Bunny in New Zealand'.

This portrait of Sydney, which accompanied the article, is a vision of Anglo-Indian respectability, a stark contrast to the rough labouring culture encountered in rural New Zealand. National Library of Scotland

ABOVE RIGHT: **MARY PATTISON**. Many Kalimpong women were placed in the comfortable homes of professional families. It was a more protected space than the men's rural settings, but in many ways more restrictive too. Sisters Mary and Kate Pattison arrived in 1915 and were initially placed in Greymouth. Both relocated to Dunedin where Mary was employed by Dr and Mrs Stewart Moody as a nanny and domestic help. Mary travelled with the family on their annual holiday to Honolulu, and she and Kate enjoyed a lifelong supportive relationship with the Moodys.

The privacy of their domestic roles meant that fewer images were taken depicting the women at work. This image of Mary Pattison with the daughter of Dr and Mrs Moody prompts consideration of the many New Zealand children who grew up in the care of Kalimpong women. Mary Milne

Jeannie Mackay married John Henderson in Dunedin, 1914.

Yvonne Gale and Jon Earley

Patrick Savigny married Dorothy Colquhoun in Scotland, 1918.

Michelle Alexander

WAR, MARRIAGE AND SETTLEMENT

World War One proved a major disruption to the emigration scheme. Shipping restrictions slowed and then halted the transport of groups to Dunedin: a party of five women arrived in 1915, after which there were no more Kalimpong emigrants until 1920. Meanwhile, almost all Kalimpong men who were fit for service volunteered and headed overseas with the New Zealand Expeditionary Force (NZEF). The anticipated pathway from farm labourer to farmer was proving problematic and, like many other labouring men, they saw war as an opportunity for adventure, travel and advancement.

War was perceived by John Graham and his graduates as a means to prove the worth of Anglo-Indians as imperial citizens. In the *Homes Magazine*, reports of the Kalimpong men who were on overseas service replaced the previous articles about emigrating groups. There were reports of Dunedin men who received military awards, and the magazine also noted the women's efforts to 'keep the home fires burning' in their domestic situations.

Although Graham had articulated an ideal pathway for men, no equivalent progression had been imagined for the women. The option had been raised of making a career of nursing, but only Molly Chambers completed this training. As it turned out, the Kalimpong women in New Zealand either remained in their positions as domestic helps and nannies, or were wed. The magazine began to carry stories that congratulated those who had married and made 'homes of their own'. The first was Jeannie Mackay, who married John Henderson in 1914.

The men also began to marry. In Scotland in 1918 Patrick Savigny married Dorothy Colquhoun, whom he met while on leave during his war service. Like all of the Kalimpong men who fought overseas, Savigny returned to New Zealand when the war was over. His story illustrates the strength of the ties that emigrants established in their early placements, and the power of the notion that New Zealand was a destination for the lucky few.

Richard May before embarking for overseas service, 1915. Harrison family

RICHARD MAY arrived in New Zealand in 1910 and worked as a farmhand in Southland before volunteering for the Otago Mounted Rifles on 20 May 1915. Bereft of contact with his birth family, Richard named a former employer, William Harrison of Dipton, Southland, as next of kin.

A few months later he wrote an affectionate letter from Egypt to William's wife Mary, expressing his gratitude to the family for all they had done for him. Richard was sent to Gallipoli soon after and was killed in action in France in September 1916.

Richard's personal effects and war medals were sent to the Harrison family. The story of his Kalimpong origins faded over time, but the family has retained his war items, letters and photographs. His story was recovered when Michelle Sim, great-great-granddaughter of William Harrison, happened to learn of my research into the Kalimpong scheme.

The Harrison family farmhouse at Grassmead, Dipton, c. 1916 with (left to right) Henry 'Harry' Parker (Carrie's future husband), Mary Harrison and Carrie Harrison. Harrison family

THE SHIFT NORTH

In 1920 the Immigration Restriction Amendment Act introduced a new system for regulating non-British migration. All individuals of non-British or Irish birth and/or parentage would now require a permit to enter New Zealand. Despite immediate consternation in Kalimpong that this would bring an end to the Homes scheme, emigrant numbers actually increased in the 1920s.

The death of James Ponder, Graham's main supporter in the south, led Graham to look to the North Island. With the assistance of Wellington barrister (and later judge) A.W. Blair, who had connections in the Customs Department and arranged permits for all arrivals in this period, several groups arrived in Wellington in the 1920s and were dispersed in the North and upper South Islands. These groups went on to establish lively and connected communities in Wellington, Auckland and Napier. Many descendants have albums full of cheerful images of the 1920s emigrants, dressed in the fashions of the time and enjoying each other's company.

But an unforeseen hurdle lay ahead. From the late 1920s, economic depression began to affect employment opportunities – especially for men, who were reliant on farm work to get started. No placements were offered for male Kalimpong emigrants after 1926, and those who had arrived in the mid-1920s suddenly found themselves out of work. In 1929 the government shut down all assisted immigration, and the scheme was put on hold.

The Depression affected the earlier generation of emigrants too, who by this time had young families to provide for but no extended family in New Zealand to turn to for support. Graham would have been pleased to learn that local families who had employed them in the past provided much-needed assistance in these difficult times.

An anxious journey. The contemplative expressions on the faces of the November 1925 group (see names in Appendix Two) reflect the uncertainty about their futures in a distant place. What lay ahead? Would they ever return to India?

Sylvia Slater (née Brooks)

From farming to forestry. Rend Mortimore and Horace Brooks, c. 1928, probably at Aplins' farm in Silverstream. As farm labour became scarce, a number of Kalimpong men banded together and worked in forestry in the central North Island. Despite the challenges of this roving existence, the men took many photographs together, displaying their good humour and hardy attitude, and sent them to the Homes Magazine.

Sylvia Slater (née Brooks)

'Eva with Champ and Betty,' from an album gifted to Eva Royston by fellow emigrant Connie Walker on her birthday in 1930. The album is brimming with photographs of Kalimpong emigrants enjoying social activities in the Wellington region. Here, Eva (centre) is likely pictured with the children she cared for in her placement with a local family.

Sylvia Slater (née Brooks)

Work–life integration. In addition to working and socialising with friends from Kalimpong, 1920s arrivals quickly forged bonds with new workmates. In this photograph, of forestry workers in Waikato, it is difficult to pick the one Kalimpong emigrant (it is Fergus Gammie, at the top of the pyramid). Gammie family

James Reid (back row, right) as secretary to Sir Frederic Truby King (centre front), 1932. Many of the men achieved a high level of education at Kalimpong, and gradually navigated their way from farm work to a more fitting place in white-collar work or owning small businesses. James Reid emigrated in 1925 and did well to attain this position by the early 1930s. He married in 1933. Ref: 1/1-018806-F, Alexander Turnbull Library, Wellington

Nancy (Annie) Dinning. Mary Milne

Violet Allcard. Mary Milne

Amy Gollan. Sylvia Slater (née Brooks)

Thomas Greig. Judi Cassidy

Charles Spalding. Spalding family

Richard Hawkins. Hawkins family

5:
A New Zealand
Community

KEEPING SIBLINGS TOGETHER

Graham encouraged tea planters to stay in touch with their children, even though he knew that many would not necessarily be willing or able to do so. His attitude to the mothers was in stark contrast: tea planters' children were to be permanently separated from their maternal families. To compensate for this intentional rupture, Graham endeavoured to keep siblings together and to facilitate their reconnections in New Zealand.

Siblings occasionally emigrated together, but since they usually reached working age at different times, the first was often sent with the promise of others to follow at a later date. Many reunions took place when new groups arrived. The majority ended up with at least one sibling in New Zealand, and some, such as the large Gammie family of Betty, Fergus, Moira, Alison, Gavin and Kathleen, had more. In light of their history of separations, having other family members nearby brought a welcome sense of connection and continuity.

These reunions did not always lead to 'happy families', however. Strict gender separation at the Homes meant that brothers and sisters often barely knew each other prior to meeting as young adults in New Zealand. Furthermore, these reunions became more difficult to effect as larger forces, such as war, made it impossible for Graham to control when a group might be sent. When the New Zealand government stopped accepting Kalimpong groups in 1929, a number of families had siblings effectively stranded in India, hopeful of later emigration.

PREVIOUS PAGES: *'Picnic at Wilton's Bush, Wellington.' A group of Kalimpong women, including the Dinning sisters Annie (centre) and Margaret (right).*
Mary Milne

TOP: *From left, Moira, Fergus and Betty Gammie.* Gammie family

ABOVE: *Siblings Mary and Thomas Greig (left and centre), with Mary's children and sister-in-law.* Judi Cassidy

LEFT: *Alice and George Peters.* McCabe family

A holiday reunion. Mary and Gwen Chaston's father took them on a trip around the South Island when he visited in the 1920s. Also present was 1912 emigrant Mae Sinclair (right). Mary Milne

TEA PLANTERS IN NEW ZEALAND

Despite the common belief that tea planters had abandoned their children to an institution that conveniently sent them to the other side of the world, some fathers of Kalimpong Kids continued to correspond with their children after they emigrated, and took an active interest in their futures. Reunions occurred too. At least five tea planters visited their children in New Zealand, and several lived out their days with their offspring.

My great-grandfather, Egerton Peters, arrived shortly after his youngest daughter Alice emigrated in 1926. Soon after this he purchased a house in Dunedin where he lived for the remaining twenty years of his life with his eldest daughter, Lorna. Another was Hugh Dinning, who followed his daughters to New Zealand. Hugh purchased an elegant villa in Karori, where the three of them occasionally hosted memorable get-togethers for the Kalimpong community. Richard Hawkins' father came to New Zealand in his old age and spent his final few years with Richard and his young family in Auckland. The Chaston sisters enjoyed a briefer reunion with their father, but still he made the effort to take them on a trip around the South Island during his 1920s visit.

How do we explain this apparent change of heart, this willingness to be reunited and seen publicly with their interracial offspring? Compared to India and Britain, New Zealand was regarded as a place of freer social relations, and was a safe distance from family and social contexts where a planter's interracial progeny might be the cause of negative gossip and rejection. As the photographic record demonstrates, a father's presence was a source of immense pride for Kalimpong people. Yet given the long period of separation and the many unanswered questions that preceded their reunions, these adult father–child relationships must surely have been somewhat strained.

Egerton Peters fishing in the Opihi River, South Canterbury, 1926. McCabe family

Hugh Dinning takes a break while travelling around the South Island with his daughters in 1938. He is pictured in Gore, where they visited Kate Wilson (née Pattison) and her young family. Mary Milne

Margaret and Annie Dinning (pictured earlier as infants in the bungalow) on holiday in the South Island with their father Hugh. The girls never married, and were fondly remembered by the Kalimpong community for their refined ways. Mary Milne

JOHN GRAHAM'S NEW ZEALAND TOUR, 1937

In July 1937 John Graham, then 75 years of age, arrived in New Zealand. He had two aims: to visit as many of his graduates as he could (by this time numbering 120), and to petition the government to restart the emigration scheme. Over three weeks he travelled the length of the country from Auckland to the Southland town of Gore and back again, going to great lengths to find those who had fallen off the radar of the Kalimpong community.

Graham left a substantial record of his visit, including two diaries – one written for the *Homes Magazine*, the other a personal account for his family that detailed the circumstances and fortunes of the Kalimpong Kids he met. He made two broadcasts on national radio and his presence was reported in newspapers all over the country. There was certainly no hushed silence around his purposeful visit.

Kalimpong people organised gatherings in each of the main centres to celebrate Graham's presence. The largest was at the residence of the Didsbury family in Wellington. The photograph of this occasion, a feature of many descendants' collections, tells us so much. The obviously well-to-do Didsburys employed a Kalimpong woman. Their social status was typical of professional Presbyterian families connected to Graham, and their hosting of this event speaks volumes about the integrated involvement of local families in the scheme. The emigrants, dressed for the occasion, display their successful transition to New Zealand life. Note that the women outnumber the men: at this time many men were still working in remote rural locations and were unable to travel to a reunion. We can also see the generations of emigrants here, with Mary Ochterlony, a 1912 emigrant seated to the left of Graham in the second row, among more recent arrivals, and the next generation (including her children) in the front row.

It must have been an amazing experience for Graham to be reunited with his former charges, who were by then reaching middle age. It certainly had a profound effect on them: a number of descendants vividly remember the excitement and emotion that his visit elicited.

OPPOSITE:
'A Wellington O.G.B's reunion at Mrs Didsbury's Residence,' 1937. This photograph and caption appeared in the Homes Magazine. *Note the presence of Janet Fraser (wife of Sir Peter Fraser), the Didsburys, Dr Graham and other employers among the Kalimpong people.*
Gammie family

FRONT ROW: Miss Duck (grandchild), Mrs Wells (Esther Graham), Connie Walker, Eva Royston, Kuki Batchelor (grandchild), Genevie Hughes (grandchild), Kate Edbrooke, Elsa Spaull, Miss McKenzie (friend), Mr Didsbury (employer).

SECOND ROW: Gwen Chaston, Mrs Duck (Rose Cooper), Mrs Didsbury, Mrs Gibson (Mary Ochterlony), Dr Graham, Mrs Stewart (Molly Chambers), Mr Roberts (friend), Mrs Fisher (Margaret Fox), Mrs Kinnear (Lucy Tweedie), Mrs Hughes (Deborah French).

THIRD ROW: Miss Duck (grandchild), Mr Newburgh (friend), Mrs Cairncross (Lucy Boden), Nell Greig, Mrs Woodmass (Mary Greig), Margaret Dinning, Mae Sinclair, Mr Dinning (father), Mr Wells (friend), Mr Duck (husband), Mrs Batchelor (Minnie Lawless), Mr Gibson (husband), Annie Dinning, Violet Allcard, Alice Smith.

BACK ROW: Mr Batchelor (husband), Lady Fraser (employer), Tom Speed, Mrs Samuel (employer), Mr Cairncross (husband), James Reid, Charles Spalding, Mr Hughes (friend), Mr Kinnear (husband), Mr Hughes' friend, Jane Mortimore, Mr Fisher (husband), Connie Speed, Rend Mortimore, Horace Brookes.

John Graham with George Langmore and his daughters Florence (left) and Gladys, Dunedin, 1937. Langmore family

GEORGE LANGMORE was born in Darjeeling and sent to the Homes in 1903, aged eight years. He arrived in Dunedin in 1911. Like all of the Kalimpong men he began as a farm labourer, but George soon secured work as an attendant at Seacliff, an asylum north of Dunedin, a position that he held for more than twenty years.

In 1918 George married Ellen Percy. He took Ellen to India in 1927, shortly after his father passed away. They visited Kalimpong and the tea estate where George was born. He is one of the few Kalimpong emigrants who ever revisited India. Several of the photographs George took on that trip are featured in this book.

By the time of John Graham's 1937 visit to New Zealand, George and Ellen had moved to the suburb of Musselburgh, in Dunedin, with their two daughters. Graham stayed with the Langmores for a week. George drove him all around the city to meet others from Kalimpong who had settled in Dunedin. In his diary Graham recorded that George 'must have done well', as his home was furnished with fine carpets from Glasgow.

Darjeeling in Dunedin. George Langmore named his house on Musselburgh Rise 'Lopchu Villa,' after his father's tea plantation in Darjeeling. Langmore family

The 1938 emigrants. Beryl Mortimer (née Radcliffe) was still alive, aged ninety-nine, at the time of writing this book. When I visited Beryl (front row, second from right) in 2014, she had a framed copy of this photograph on her wall. See Appendix Two for the names of the others in this group. Gammie family

1938: THE FINAL GROUP

Despite Graham's hopes that Kalimpong Kids could be settled in all parts of the British Empire, New Zealand was the only settler colony that ever accepted groups from the Homes. Graham was convinced by his meetings with government officials in 1937 – including acting Prime Minister Peter Fraser – that his charges could once again emigrate to what he described as 'the best place in the world for the boys and girls of Kalimpong.' And indeed, after a little bureaucratic to-and-froing, the 1938 group was on its way.

Among the arrivals were Kathleen and Gavin Gammie, whose four siblings had emigrated in the 1920s. Kathleen and Gavin had left the Homes several years earlier and been placed in India as a temporary measure, in the hope that the emigration scheme would resume. Another reunion saw Thornton Kennedy join his sister Jessie, who was by then married with two small children. One of those children, Jim Twist, remembered the group arriving and spoke of his boyish delight at this boost to his extended family: not only with the addition of his 'real' uncle, Thornton, but with a whole batch of new 'uncles' and 'aunties,' as the Kalimpong people were fondly known.

Because the scheme was halted between 1929 and 1938, the Homes training had moved away from farming and towards clerical work, which Anglo-Indians tended to be employed for in India. The men in the 1938 group sent to New Zealand were still placed as farm workers, however, and many struggled with this transition. Their difficulties were quickly resolved by the outbreak of World War Two. Within a year of arriving, the majority would be serving in the NZEF.

In an equally sudden turn of events, and to Graham's great disappointment, this was to be the final group sent from Kalimpong to New Zealand. In 1939 the government rejected the next application for permits, stating that no further Anglo-Indians would be allowed to enter. The reason? Mixed-race people, the department advised, were 'undesirable.'

Colin Bayley on the farm at Peka Peka, shortly after arrival in 1938. Bayley family

Colin Bayley enlisted in 1941 and served overseas with the 25th Battalion. Bayley family

COLIN BAYLEY arrived with the 1938 group and went straight to work on a farm at Peka Peka. From there he went to Bothamleys' farm at Porirua before signing up for war service. He was captured in June 1942 and spent the rest of his service as a prisoner of war in Italy. After the war he completed a two-year training course in carpentry through the Rehabilitation Department, and went on to spend most of his working life at General Motors.

Colin and his wife Violet settled in Stokes Valley and had two children. Their son Steven remembers visits from other Kalimpong people who lived in the valley, including Sylvia (the flowergirl), who has contributed many photographs for this book.

Colin Bayley married Violet Holt on 18 August 1951. The bridesmaid and best man – siblings Nancy and Jim Twist – were the children of 1920s emigrant Jessie Twist (née Kennedy). The flowergirl is Sylvia Brooks, whose parents Connie Walker and Horace Brooks were both from Kalimpong. Bayley family

The Nicholls family on the farm, 1950s. When the Kalimpong scheme was halted in 1938, only the eldest of Frank Nicholls' children, Sheila, had been sent to New Zealand. Frank took matters into his own hands, purchasing a farm in the North Island and escorting his children there one by one as they reached the end of their education at Kalimpong. Left to right: Ruth, Sidney, Sheila and Norah Nicholls. *Ruth den Boogert (née Nicholls)*

6: Across Borders

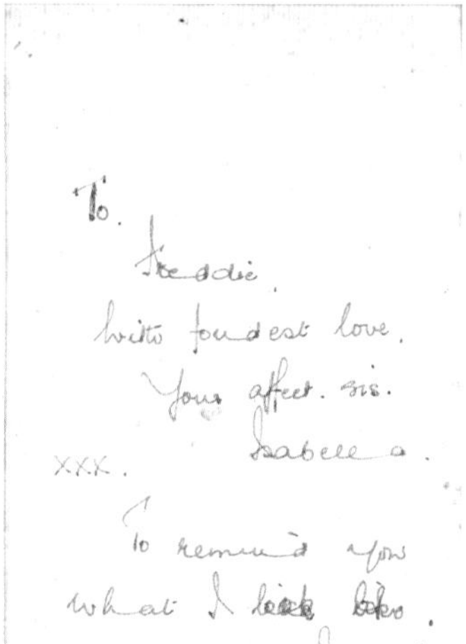

To.
Freddie.
with fondest love.
Your affect. sis.
Isabella.
XXX.

To remind you
what I look like.
Isabel.

LEFT: *Isabella Gammie (née Leith) served as an auxiliary nurse in the Indian Army before emigrating to New Zealand in 1947, just before Indian independence. She sent this photograph to her brother Fred with an affectionate note inscribed on the verso: 'To remind you what I look like.'* *Gammie family*

ABOVE: *Fred Leith (right) on his wedding day, 1 December 1945, with his best man, an army friend known as 'wee Mac.' According to his son, Fred forgot to pick up his suit, and happily donned his war uniform instead. He married Joan Hay at Knox Church, Miramar.* *Leith family*

SERVING AGAIN: WORLD WAR TWO

Like the early emigrants who had enthusiastically volunteered for service in World War One, when war was declared in 1939 the next generation of Kalimpong men – and this time, women too – seized the opportunity to prove their worth. Photographs of proud emigrants in uniform are testament to their contribution, social integration and successes in military service. Thanks to military training received at Kalimpong and their disciplined upbringing, the men excelled in war duties, which brought opportunities for white-collar work upon their return.

Fred Leith was a high achiever at the Homes and had trained as an accountant before being offered a berth with the 1938 group. Upon arrival in Wellington he was dismayed to find himself placed on a farm where he lived in a 'shack' with other farm workers. He had just begun to make inroads into finding more appropriate employment when war was declared. Fred wasted no time in signing up, and credited his disciplined upbringing with instilling the values and resilience that helped him to cope with the challenges of war. He later told his son that war service had been the highlight of his life.

Fred was not alone in this sentiment. Several of the men who had fought in World War One volunteered again in 1939. Richard Hawkins, a 1920s emigrant, made lifelong friendships during his service and secured a farm through the ballot scheme for returned serviceman – making him one of the few who achieved the goal that Graham originally envisaged for the Kalimpong men. William Beaton ended his reflective memoir (see Appendix One) by stating that war was the one time in his life that he experienced deep friendship.

THE IMPACT OF INDIAN INDEPENDENCE

In addition to the global impact of World War Two, the 1940s was a decade of upheaval in India, and this had ripple effects in former British colonies, including New Zealand. When John Graham visited in 1937 he spoke of the inevitability of Indian independence, and the need for the Dominion to accord the people of India their rightful place in the British Empire or suffer the consequences when India gained autonomy. Graham died in 1942, halfway through World War Two and five years before India gained independence from Britain in 1947.

With the end of the emigration scheme in 1938, followed by Graham's death and then India's independence, there was enormous uncertainty about the continued existence of the Homes. After all, it was a Scottish institution set up for the children of British tea planters. What place did it have in an India without the British? The Kalimpong community in New Zealand worried about the future of the school where they grew up, but increasingly felt that India no longer had any relevance for them. There seemed little hope of the emigration scheme ever being revived.

Despite this, many of the New Zealanders retained regular contact with their friends and relations from the Homes who had been placed in India and who, like many Anglo-Indians in India in the 1940s, began to make urgent enquiries about emigrating due to the uncertainty of their status once the British left. Some wrote to their New Zealand kin asking for sponsorship to emigrate. This wasn't an easy request to fulfil, and occasionally led to tensions between those still in India and those settled in New Zealand. For a number of individuals, however, these connections did facilitate emigration, and emotional reunions followed.

An esteemed visitor. Gandhi visits Dr Graham's Homes at Kalimpong, c. 1946. Ruth den Boogert (née Nicholls)

PARALLEL LIVES

While some Kalimpong graduates placed in India attempted to join their kin in New Zealand, others emigrated to Britain, and others still to Australia as immigration regulations there were relaxed. Many stayed in India. The New Zealanders were unique in being part of an organised migration scheme, but they were also part of a widely dispersed global community of Kalimpongites.

The lives these young people forged for themselves in different parts of the world raise questions about alternative pathways they might have followed. Though social opportunity was relatively limited in India, there were advantages to staying there. Graduates placed in India could visit the Homes quite easily, and there was a better chance of seeking out their mothers, which many did in later life. Those who went to Britain achieved the dream of going 'home' that was common to many Anglo-Indians, but their memoirs portray a difficult transition to a place where they were 'just Indians': their identity, so unique in India, counted for little in Britain.

Many descendants have ended up with photographs of these scattered friends whose identities and connections to the New Zealanders are completely lost. Their presence in family albums is an arresting reminder of the different worlds inhabited by graduates, and of the unseen aspects of the Kalimpong people's lives, many details of which we will never know. But this can be viewed in a positive light. Our forebears are entitled to retain some mystery after all; and speculating about unknown people in albums at least ensures our ongoing engagement with this history.

Descendants' engagement with the photographic record perhaps also belies a kind of ordinary 'Orientalism'. Alluring images, and the lost identities and stories of the individuals portrayed, have engendered a fascination that has contributed to the survival of these photographs of strangers.

ABOVE: *Unknown Kalimpong women in India. This photograph is part of the extensive collection that Judi Cassidy inherited from her great-aunt, Janet Greig.* Judi Cassidy

RIGHT: *Charles Savigny (front), the brother of New Zealand emigrant Patrick Savigny, with a friend, in India. When Patrick died in 1951, his son wrote to the Homes enquiring as to the whereabouts of Charles.* Michelle Alexander

THE HOUSEMOTHERS: AN ENDURING PRESENCE

The housemothers who volunteered at the Homes came from all corners of the British Empire. Their role in the cottages was all-encompassing: as de facto mothers they oversaw the provision of food and clothing, meted out discipline and trained children in household chores – all the while trying to keep control of up to forty children who ranged in age from five to fifteen. It must have been a challenging role. Housemothers made a lasting impression on their charges, and being on their good side made an enormous difference to a child's life in the cottages. Former Homes children recalled both difficult and affectionate housemothers, and stories abound of the pranks played on them.

A number of housemothers were New Zealanders. Mary Kennedy, for example, set out from Dunedin in 1908 under the auspices of the Presbyterian Church to volunteer at Kalimpong. She was at the Homes for at least five years and chaperoned emigrant groups to Dunedin. She married after returning to New Zealand permanently and, like other returned housemothers, her home became a place for welcoming new arrivals from Kalimpong. My grandmother, Lorna Peters, retained a lifelong friendship with Mary – yet Lorna's own family had no idea that Mary was connected to her Indian upbringing.

Little is known about the motivation, experience or length of service of these women, but, like the tea planters, they have left a visual record of their time in India. Peg Olsen, who lived in Hastings and kept in contact with a number of Kalimpong graduates, had several albums of her time as a housemother in Kalimpong. After her death, Peg's husband gifted these albums to Isabella and Gavin Gammie, whose daughter Anne Beckett now has them. The albums reveal the housemothers' adventures in greater India, their concern for children in their care, and their enduring presence among the Kalimpong community in New Zealand.

Staff at Dr Graham's Homes. From Peg Olsen's album: Peg is seated in the front row, far right. Gammie family

Aunty Barbara, Elliot Cottage housemother. From Connie Walker's collection. Sylvia Slater (née Brooks)

Housemothers adventuring in the Himalayan region. From Peg Olsen's album. Gammie family

Peg Olsen (left) is pictured here with the bride Isabella Gammie (née Leith) and Joan Leith, who had recently married Isabella's brother Fred. This airy snapshot is a wonderful expression of the intricate bonds that wove the community together.
Leith family

'THE WEDDING'. On New Year's Day 1950 Peg Olsen wrote a delightful letter to staff at the Homes, describing the marriage of two 'Kalimpongites', Gavin Gammie and Isabella Leith, at St Stephen's Presbyterian Church in Wellington. Peg named twenty former pupils among the guests at the wedding, saying it imparted 'a real Kalimpong atmosphere'. 'I'll never forget the reception they gave to an old Auntie of Kalimpong,' she wrote, adding that it made it all worthwhile 'to see their faces, and the reality of their appreciation'.

Morning tea with the governor-general. On Saturday 30 July 1966, Kalimpong emigrants in the Wellington region attended morning tea at Government House, by invitation of Sir Bernard Fergusson (pictured front with Lady Fergusson). Fergusson had military experience in India, but his connection to the Kalimpong community is not known. *Gammie family*

7: Twilight Years

Kalimpong emigrants with their spouses and children at Jim Gammie's christening, 1951.

BACK ROW (LEFT TO RIGHT): *Horace Brooks, Isabella Gammie, Bubbles Kinnear, May [last name unknown], Bob Kinnear, Violet Bayley, Colin Bayley, Amy Gollan, Dave Kinnear, Shirley Kinnear, Gavin Gammie, Connie Brooks, Hamish Tweedie.*

FRONT ROW (LEFT TO RIGHT): *George Hall, Fred Leith (with son John), Joan Leith (with son Martin), Lucy Kinnear, Betty Hall, Sylvia Brooks, Kath Tweedie.* *Gammie family*

LEAVING THE PAST BEHIND

By the 1950s the Kalimpong people were focused on their lives in New Zealand, with growing families, businesses to run and involvement in community activities. As India turned sharply away from its relationship with Britain, public interest in its fortunes began to decline. In this context the story of their Indian heritage began to fade. There is no doubt that Kalimpong people wanted to protect their children from the trauma of their past. Raised to be ashamed of their Indian heritage, it is understandable that they did not want to speak of it.

Still, they made time to get together and wrote to each other with news of family milestones and of other Kalimpong people in their area. One memorable gathering for the community in Wellington was the christening of Jim Gammie in 1951. Jim was the first child of Gavin and Isabella Gammie (née Leith). Their marriage – and several others between Kalimpong emigrants – forged lasting ties across family lines and helps to explain the strength of the Wellington community. The group photograph of Jim's christening is a favourite among the descendants of the emigrants depicted in it.

Remarkably, there is a copy of this photograph in the National Library of Scotland's 'Kalimpong Papers', a collection of archival materials relating to John Graham. The placement of letters and photographs in a public archive alerts us to the lack of privacy for those involved in this organised scheme. But the photograph's presence in the library is also evidence of the lifelong bonds formed at Kalimpong. It was most likely sent with a letter to James Purdie, long-time secretary at the Homes and a prolific and much-loved correspondent with Kalimpong graduates all over the world.

Blending in. In urban and rural settings alike, the children of the Kalimpong emigrants blended effortlessly into New Zealand society, as Graham had hoped.

OPPOSITE: *The three sons of Molly (née Chambers) and John Stewart, outside their home in Rongotai Terrace, Wellington, c. 1940. Left to right: Ian, Clyde and Malcolm.* Stewart family

ABOVE: *Bruce and Judi, grandchildren of Mary (née Greig) and Alan Woodmass, on holiday from Auckland at the family farm in Levin.* Judi Cassidy

PLANTERS' BEQUESTS

Just as relationships with housemothers and friends endured, so too did contact with tea planters. Reunions in New Zealand may have been the exception, but many Kalimpong people maintained a correspondence with their fathers. Although most were reluctant to approach the British branch of their family – anticipating rejection or awkwardness at best – the occasion of their father's death did prompt some to make contact, their thoughts naturally turning to whether or not they would inherit a share of his estate.

The question of inheritance brings us back to those romantic notions of the wealthy tea planter. The disparity between the modest lives of Kalimpong people in New Zealand and the presumed wealth of tea planters led many descendants to wonder, 'What happened to all the money?' As noted earlier, a tea planter was the manager of an estate, employed by a tea agency, and seldom had a financial stake in a plantation. While they enjoyed a comfortable lifestyle, they weren't paid a large amount. But descendants were not to know this; their impressions were shaped by nostalgic images and a powerful colonial stereotype.

A number of planters did make bequests to their children. Tom Spalding, a 1920s emigrant, moved from farm labouring to working as a mechanic in Awanui, a small town in the Far North. When Tom's father passed away, many years earlier, he left money in a trust with the Homes, to be given to his children when they reached adulthood. (Notably, he also made provision for the mother of his children, which was unusual.) With the money from his father's estate, Tom purchased a house and land just outside Awanui town centre; he built a workshop on the property and opened his own garage in 1943. The business grew, and when the Awanui service station came up for sale in 1950, Tom purchased it and opened Spalding's Garage.

Spalding's Garage, Awanui. Given the importance of a garage in a remote rural town, ownership of this business facilitated full immersion into the community for Tom Spalding and his family. Spalding family

Patrick Savigny relaxing on the beach in Dunedin. Michelle Alexander

Mary Woodmass (née Greig) at home in Levin. Judi Cassidy

RETIREMENT

The early lives of Kalimpong emigrants were punctuated by sudden family separations, journeys into the unknown, and long periods of transition. Perhaps unsurprisingly then, the photographic record of their adult lives shows them revelling in domestic contentment. They eased gracefully into the latter stages of their lives, relaxing at home, participating in family get-togethers with children and grandchildren, and enjoying hobbies like gardening and playing bowls. Very few ever travelled beyond New Zealand after making the journey from Kalimpong. Having forged a place for themselves, they were reluctant to risk starting again in a context where their status would be uncertain.

Kalimpong Kids had arrived on British passports, and because New Zealand citizenship was not enacted until the late 1940s, there was no clear route to formalising their residency. In later years when a birth certificate was required to apply for a pension, most solved the problem by writing to the Homes to obtain a copy of their baptism certificate. These letters were added to their files, and descendants who visited Kalimpong were surprised to find that their parent or grandparent had re-established contact with the Homes in relatively recent times.

The Kalimpong people enjoyed affectionate relationships with us, their children and grandchildren, and this is expressed in our respect for the sensitivity surrounding their Indian heritage. Our eventual discovery of the Kalimpong story, and the reasons for their secrecy and silence, has been a source of wonder, sadness and confusion. We understand the stigma of race and illegitimacy, but we don't quite understand the reasons for preventing the next generations from knowing anything about their ancestry. Those of us who have visited Kalimpong wonder how they could have lived in two such different worlds and managed to hold it all in.

TOP LEFT: *Molly (née Chambers) and John Stewart at their son Malcolm's wedding in Lower Hutt, March 1958.* Stewart family

TOP RIGHT: *Lorna McCabe (née Peters), Pine Hill, Dunedin, 1970s. Lorna's father emigrated to New Zealand and purchased this property in 1926, where they ran a small poultry farm.* McCabe family

RIGHT: *Kate Wilson (née Pattison), Christchurch, c. 1960. Kate's house was a gathering place for local Kalimpong people, as was her home in Dunedin many years earlier.* Mary Milne

ABOVE: *Jeannie Henderson (née McKay) in St Kilda, Dunedin, 1960s. Jeannie sewed for Hallenstein Bros for several years, and accumulated several thousand shares in the company in later life.* Yvonne Gale

Rose Cooper and Mary Ochterlony arrived with the 1912 group. Mary was initially placed in Blenheim, and Rose in rural Otago. By the 1920s they were both living in the Wellington region, where they remained good friends as each married and had children.

ABOVE: *Four generations. Rose Duck (née Cooper) holds her great-grandson Shayne, with her daughter Olive Affleck (left) and granddaughter Dianne Ryder (right).*

Ryder family

LEFT: *Mary Gibson (née Ochterlony, seated) celebrated her 101st birthday on 23 September 1996 with her three children in Levin. Left to right: Olive Woolley, James Gibson and Alison Ratcliffe.* *Steve and Glenis Woolley*

Renée Pearson, descendant of 1914 emigrant Henry Holder, in Langtang Valley, Nepal, two days before the devastating earthquake of April 2015. Renée missed her planned visit to Kalimpong, but fortunately made it home safely. Renée Pearson

8: *The Next Generation*

DR GRAHAM'S HOMES IN THE 21ST CENTURY

When India gained independence in 1947, it was thought that British institutions like the Homes in Kalimpong had no future. The Homes did survive, but only after some immediate changes were agreed to: the name of the institution was changed from St Andrew's Colonial Homes to Dr Graham's Homes, and Bengali replaced English as the language of instruction. Other changes took longer. The last of the British tea planters did not leave India until the 1970s, and the Homes continued to take in their mixed-race children right to the end.

The institution today is a busy place with over 1400 students, some of whom reside in the same cottages that the Kalimpong emigrants to New Zealand lived in, so many years ago. There are still a number of Anglo-Indian children from cities like Kolkata in residence, and the Homes operate a sponsorship programme that sees it retain a measure of its original charitable aims. It is regarded as a good school at which to obtain an English education, and is attended by local day-pupils as well as fee-paying boarders from all over India and other parts of Asia. The curriculum has broadened to reflect the cultural diversity of its pupils.

Through all of these changes, the personal files created for every student admitted since 1900 have been carefully preserved. When I visited in 2007 it took archivist Ruth Glashan only a few minutes to locate my grandmother's file, untouched for a hundred years, even though I had very little information to offer. It was an unexpected and precious moment. A decade later the same sense of discovery awaited Chelsea Dolman. It is an ever-unfolding story.

In the office of Dr Graham's Homes, my great-grandmother's file was plonked into my hands. A wave of emotion hit me and the staff stared at me as I burst into tears. I wasn't sad, I was just overwhelmed by the idea that such a detailed and important aspect of my family's history had been sitting alone on a dusty shelf waiting, all this time. Thank goodness for Mrs Ruth Glashan and her comforting offer of tea.

I didn't know my great-grandmother, but after spending time back in New Zealand transcribing the many letters and documents with my mum, I now have a much clearer picture of the wonderful woman she was, the precious early years she spent at Dr Graham's Homes, and the special connection she kept with the school throughout her life.

—Chelsea Dolman

Searching for Lorna. The author at Kalimpong, November 2007, looking for her grandmother's name in the admissions book. Author

Chelsea Dolman (right), great-granddaughter of Mary Roberts, with Ruth Glashan, the Homes archivist, in 2016. Chelsea Dolman

LEFT: *Wolseley House, the former principal's residence, where the author stayed on her research visit in 2012. Like all of the cottages, it is nestled in trees down a winding path.* ABOVE: *Path to Woodburn Cottage. Author*

Hart Cottage. Author

Descendants who visit the Homes today are moved by the experience of being in the space where their forebears grew up: touching a stair rail, feeling the wooden floor beneath their feet or sitting on a bed. Little has changed in the cottages (or other school buildings) since the 1920s.

ABOVE: *The dormitory in Woodburn Cottage, where Lorna Peters slept for fifteen years.* Author

LEFT: *Hart Cottage interior.* Author

A COMMUNITY REVIVED

Descendants of Kalimpong Kids have been travelling to India since the 1980s in a bid to uncover the story of their parent's or grandparent's past. The earliest descendants to make the journey did so without the many benefits of the internet, and faced frequent disruptions due to political agitation by local groups seeking greater autonomy from the Indian government. The lengths descendants have gone to in order to visit Kalimpong attest to the importance of the quest to know one's family history, especially where details have been withheld or lost.

This desire for knowledge has been spurred on in recent decades by the increasing ease of travel and research, and the broad impetus to reconnect broken family pasts, which of course is not limited to the Kalimpong community. The twentieth century was characterised by global upheavals, migration, and subsequent well-meaning attempts to shield the next generation from fraught family histories. People today want to put the pieces back together, and reuniting families across borders has been a crucial means of achieving this in a personal and meaningful way. Photographs have enabled such reunions in myriad ways.

Alongside this spirit of reconnection there has developed a desire for social interactions where formerly taboo subjects may be openly discussed. When I began my doctoral research in 2011, I looked for descendants to be part of the study. Many of those I found had, like me, been to Kalimpong and retrieved a copy of their family file, which they were willing to share. They also had photographs, and these began to coalesce in my mind into a visual history. Upon completion of my PhD, I held an event in Dunedin for descendants at which I hoped to reignite the spirit of the reunions held when John Graham visited in 1937. Though most of us were meeting for the first time, there was a sense of ease, of something in common – something difficult to articulate but wonderful to experience.

Memorable meetings with descendants on my first research trip in 2011.
TOP LEFT: *Sylvia Slater (née Brooks) and Anne Beckett (née Gammie) in Upper Hutt.*
TOP RIGHT: *Siblings Ian Spalding and Margaret Matterson (née Spalding) in Auckland.* Author

At the 2014 reunion in Dunedin.
LOWER LEFT: *Anne Beckett (left) discusses photographs with Pam and Peter Gardiner and Anthony Mortimore (front).*
LOWER RIGHT: *David Coe (pictured left with his wife Annette) travelled from Australia to reunite with his South Island cousins, Anthony Mortimore, Maree Harper, Gavin Mortimore and Jan Ogilvy, who all grew up in Invercargill.* Chris Ward

Kalimpong descendants have reunited with branches of their families in Britain and India. This photograph records a special moment in 2009 when Jim Gammie met his aunt, Alexa Bibby (née Gammie), in England. Alexa missed joining her six siblings when the scheme to New Zealand was halted in 1938. She married a British soldier in India and made a life in England with him, never to see her siblings again. Gammie family

Kalimpong descendant Gilbert Hawkins with his wife Annette in a village in Assam in 2012. Along with Gilbert's sister Pam and her husband Peter Gardiner, the families have made two journeys to Kalimpong – the second time venturing further afield to the tea-planting districts of far northeast Assam, where they located the plantation on which their father Richard was born. *Hawkins family*

Kalimpong reunion, 2014: a two-day event that brought seventy descendants to Dunedin to meet and share stories. Most travelled from the North Island. Chris Ward

Upper Hutt, 2017. Our second national gathering was held at Upper Hutt College – an appropriate location in light of the many Kalimpong families that settled in the Hutt Valley. Chris Ward

On the beach in Varkala, Kerala, India. Molly Chambers' granddaughter Andrea Stewart and her partner Ross Vintiner with their two beautiful daughters adopted from Pune, India – Zeenat (left) and Sazia (right). The family has returned to India many times to celebrate the girls' culture and heritage. Zeenat and Sazia have a special connection with Molly as they share her birthday, 24 April. Stewart family

THE JOURNEY CONTINUES

Andrea Stewart is the granddaughter of Molly Chambers, who arrived in New Zealand in 1915. Molly was the only Kalimpong emigrant to train as a nurse. She married and settled in Wellington. As noted earlier, Andrea's initial research into her grandmother's heritage in the 1990s was made difficult by Molly's assertion that the school she attended in India had burnt down. Andrea eventually found her way to Kalimpong where she uncovered the story of Molly's upbringing and her pathway to New Zealand.

This motivation to know more about her grandmother's origins stemmed in part from Andrea and her partner Ross's desire to adopt from India. At the time, there was a better chance of achieving this if one had a family connection to India. Having established this connection on her trip to Kalimpong in 1999, Andrea and Ross went through an intercountry process to adopt sisters Zeenat and Sazia. Both girls had been orphaned as infants and have no knowledge of their parents. At the descendants' reunion in Dunedin in 2014 the girls were at times a little overcome with emotion as they heard echoes of their own familial separations in the Kalimpong stories shared that day. Their story is a good reminder that children everywhere continue to be separated from their parents and their ancestry.

This photograph opens up an opportunity to reflect upon the continuous unfolding of the Kalimpong story, and the multiple ways of realigning and reconnecting with our histories. The beach could be in New Zealand or India, though it could not be at Kalimpong, where an unforgettable mountain scene frames the landscape. Kalimpong Kids first saw the ocean when they stepped onto the ship that would take them away from the only home they had known: India.

The restless ocean serves as a metaphor for the undercurrents of life and ancestry that move us back and forth in our quest to make sense of our family histories. Finding acceptance is akin to letting the waves of what we know and what we may never know wash over us, allowing ourselves to be drawn into the current, to be carried somewhere that enables us to view things from a different perspective: to look back, to look ahead, and to find comfort in the unceasing magnetic pull of family.

Appendices

William Beaton as school captain (above), and in his athletics uniform (right), Kalimpong, 1938. Beaton family

APPENDIX ONE: WILLIAM BEATON'S MEMOIR

William (Bill) Beaton arrived in New Zealand with the 1938 group from Kalimpong and enlisted in the army soon after. He was initially sent to Fiji to face the potential threat of Japanese invasion, then was accepted into the air force and qualified as a fighter pilot. After the war he established a top-dressing company and later worked as a sales manager. He and his wife Norma (née Buckley) had four children.

According to his son Ian, Bill regarded his immigration as a success but 'kept his memories of India close to his chest and did not like being questioned about his early life'. Ian and his wife Loma visited Kalimpong in 1980. Their visit raised many questions for them about Bill's upbringing; when approached, however, he 'clammed up' in response.

A decade later, at Loma's request, Bill wrote a memoir of his experiences in India – from early life on the tea plantation and his difficult transition to Kalimpong to his departure for New Zealand. It was a revelation to Ian – an intimate glimpse into aspects of his father's life that had been long hidden.

Bill died in 2002 and is buried at Nga Potiki station.

The following excerpts from William Beaton's memoir have been lightly edited.

... **AS CAN BE GUESSED** I was an unashamed loner – I could never recall, in all my years at school, anyone whom I could call my friend. It was a strange affliction related probably to my young years when I adopted this horrible attitude to keep my own problems to myself. I was friendly to all, but never a friend to anyone, and no one knew my innermost person – possibly only my family, of whom my wife knew only what she required to stick by me in close association since 1940, to her untimely death in 1986. But she was one in a million, and for the rest of my broad family I am writing all this – may they get an insight to 'Dad-Grandad'.

...

I was born on 5 October 1920, the first of three children to Domoya and William S. Beaton – their other children were brother James and sister Elizabeth. My place of birth was Namdang Tea Estate with Margherita as the main township. My recollection of Margherita is of the railway station situated a few hundred yards beyond the township, which snuggled in a hollow just beyond the last piers of the railway bridge which spanned a river the size of the Ruamahanga.[1] My memory is still vivid, of gazing from my railway carriage at many of the crocodiles laying on the sandbanks located mid-stream. Meanwhile *dhobis* (washerwomen/men) carried out their cleaning tasks on the riverbank. Assam was similar to other Indian regions.

The enclave Margherita occupied was typical of a thousand Indian market towns – thriving activity, buying and trading. The incessant thump, thump of the oil wells of the Burma Oil Company, and the continuous shunting of rail wagons, busy loading coal from nearby fields, indicated that this was a vital hive of industrial activity to the British/Indian government of those days.

I was born in the bungalow very close to the tea factory. The bungalow was a thatched-roof abode such as found in Devon or Cornwall. The path leading out to the back section had a pineapple garden and was infested with snakes, and I often wondered who harvested the fruit. I remember playing in the shed when a large cobra was entwining itself in the A-frame of the shed above my head. My brother James was born in that house, and my next recollection was of being snatched from a bath, outside, to watch my father futilely trying to put out a blazing fire that enveloped the house. I remember my mother drying me and panicking, as did literally the dozens of Indians observing the scene. We completely lost that home and contents.

By then I was over three years old and we found ourselves in a huge complex as a temporary residence. This residential area was primarily for newcomer European planters – there were English, Scots, and an Australian planter, who thought I was nice to say the least. I could not walk, or refused to walk and resorted to hopping like a frog. Hence my nickname 'Beng', which meant frog.

...

I must have been five or six years old when my mother lay in agony after recurring pains. My father summoned this fakir or witch doctor – call him what you like. After a lot of mumbo-jumbo he put his mouth on her stomach/side, sucked, and then spat out a couple of stones into a receptacle. Gall stones? Kidney stones? I know he made no incision and also she was up and about in next to no time. I lay in bed soon after this time with raging malaria despite the plantation's doctor from the Estate hospital. No amount of quinine (bitter) or sponging down could quell my raging temperature, or ease the boiling hot/ice-cold spells I experienced. The fakir came. The concoction he prepared in a vessel he made me drink with help from father and mother. The malaria, which was a killer in those regions, just vanished, never to return to me.

...

My mother was a Gurkha, but I do not think she came from Nepal, but rather from the Terai region on the slopes of the Himalayas. Where and when my father met her I do not know, but her immediate family had a house on the banks of the Brahmaputra (India's biggest river). I was taken there when 3–5 years young to a property rather lavish compared to other Indian homes. Somewhat like homes in Queensland built on stilts. Vague memories of bananas, pawpaws, jackfruit, lychees and a host of other tropical fruits with flying foxes (fruit bats) openly gorging themselves. I spent my time about 300 yards away from this home on the banks of a small, deep river watching wild elephants stripping branches from trees in nearby jungle, or blowing bubbles from a type of castor oil plant that excreted a milky fluid which gave fantastic rainbow-coloured bubbles.

My mother was pretty and very petite. A reasonably light skin with no indication of any Mongolian features. She dressed to the hilt with her trim figure, and I don't think I ever saw her in other dresses but saris of the finest quality. Only her night attire was European. Her jewellery seemed to be aplenty and her adaption to the lifestyle afforded by my father suited her entirely. Her *ayah* (attendant female) obeyed every whim of my mother, which probably indicated the hate and jealousy the servants, as a whole, harboured for this female who literally behaved as a 'ranee'[2] mem-sahib in her association with them. She ruled the roost, and my father could not have cared less. What an amalgamation of Scottish/Gurhka association!

We enjoyed a good family atmosphere at that stage. We were happy like a good NZ family – very much like a happy family here.

...

I remember a safari into the very heart of the Naga country with my father. There were bearers, tents, spirit lamps, fishing rods, as we trudged and hacked our way through to this beautiful, silent, deep river in the back of nowhere. His prime object was to get Mahseer, a renowned fighting fish and prized for its delicacy. I remember fondly a Tilly lamp, camp stools, his slow sipping of his *chota-pegs* (drinks) and my allocation of an ice-cold beer from the cooling river, and most important of all a huge dinner of steaming hot prawn curry. This Scot was never an emotional man and we communed in silence. I guess in his own way he helped to shape my own manhood – the porridge, haggis, whiskey, the mists of his Highlands! The trumpeting of the wild elephants and bark of the howler monkeys kept us aware of jungle activities throughout, although father appeared to sleep peacefully.

...

My father went away for three months. My mother looked after our very destinies at this time. If she was unpopular prior to my father's furlough, she now became unbearable to her personal female attendant, and to the servants in general. In short, my mother started playing up – committing adultery. I remember some slimy beggar occupying my father's favourite recliner, and smoking his cigarettes. Indians are observant – add fuel to the fire and all hell will ultimately break loose. It did upon my father's return. The reunion was quite normal, the usual gifts he brought back. It was evening, and we shared what transpired to be the last family gathering.

That night a cavalcade of torch-wielding Indians descended upon us. As I lay in bed (I could speak fluent Hindi) I heard the saga of hate and recriminations surface from them – they branded my mother for all her misdeeds. All this went on to the early hours of the morning, my father turning his wrath on my mother. After she had packed, us kids were woken up (if we slept!) and summoned to the sitting room. Things were calmer even if my mother still wept. Her insistence on being with her kids – nil. My father said he could only look after a 'Beng'. Then my world collapsed. I cried for days and days for my mother, brother and sister.

It was never the same for me again. Thus began my lifestyle adaption which, I know, is still the reason why I'm inwardly such a loner – circumstances dictated my early life, and the pattern thus set cannot be easily erased.

...

When the time arrived for my departure to St Andrew's, Kalimpong, our cook, the tall striking Pathan, was given the task. He absolutely mollycoddled me every inch of the journey. Dressed in his flowing robes, turban, dagger etc., he must have struck a note of caution to any impending intruder. We stayed the night in Siliguri before embarking on the toy Darjeeling train. Finally he delivered me to Mr Purdie, who was Dr Graham's second-in-command. I remember this huge man bowing in front of me as a farewell and saying his Muslim blessing, 'Allah be with you *chota sahib*.' I subsequently wondered what the staunch Presbyterian Mr Purdie thought of this?

Thus began my formal schooling and it was a cultural shock to one who grew up in the extremes of civilisation up to this age of nine. From the outset I felt I was in a strange, hostile, and distinctly unfriendly environment to that which I was accustomed – I had never met so many young boys of my own age at the one time. No one greeted me or endeavoured any act of friendliness or welcome on that first day in school. That evening we were given the usual meal of three slices of bread and butter/jam for small boys, six slices for older boys, soup and cocoa. Then followed evening prayers, to be followed by homework for those allocated some and bed for the youngest.

No little boy ever sobbed so silently into his pillow every night for the first few weeks. I wept for my home a thousand miles away. My father, the renewed memories of my mother, brother, sister, my freedom, rifle, bike etc. etc., even the household dogs, cat and even my pet mongoose. Also the servants, horses, general atmosphere as compared to this strange much colder clime situation (4500ft elevation). Notice my reference to silent sobbing – you got thrashed if you indulged in such unmanly behaviour! In my first few weeks I was hit often, probably due to my tendency to withdraw into my shell as a form of self-protection, but this was of little comfort.

• • •

If the 'rule of the jungle' did not actually exist, it was certainly the strongest who ruled the weakest. Names etched in my memory were those of Harding, Banyard, Wilson, and only Hedley Myers could be called a decent older boy – the rest were bullying swines who made the younger boys' lives utterly miserable. In fairness, not always, as we soon learnt to disappear or keep completely out of their paths! Miss Sparrow was a kind-hearted matron whose reputation extended throughout the school. She endeavoured to keep an eye on most things, but even in those days this over-religious old maid tended to ignore events so vital to our wellbeing.

Going home to the plantation for my Christmas holidays resulted in a great welcome from my father, and a riotous greeting from the three dogs Jean and Jet – spaniels – and the bitterly jealous Sidney terrier Sam, who considered me his personal property. The monkey, who ran the length of the verandah railings, eyed me with renewed suspicion (the bugger used to bite!) and the talking mynahs and the parrots carried on their usual activities. The assembled entourage of staff – bearers, cook, kitchen hand, gardener, stable groom – gave me a smiling reception for the little sahib was a welcome figure to break their monotony. I got on well with them.

During my last years at St Andrew's I became an avid collector of exotic tropical butterflies – my absolute passion, to which I devoted any spare time away from studies and sports. I made my own catching nets and glass/wood display, and brought the quite outstanding collection with me to New Zealand. I donated them to the Dominion Museum, and I often wonder if they are still there as 'tropical butterflies'?

. . .

My last experience of the 'occult' in this mysterious India. I was within a few feet of climbing the gangway to board the SS *Strathmore* with the twelve others emigrating to New Zealand. This swami, guru, brushed his way past everyone and pulled me up. He insisted, persisted, on reading my palm – no payment, he said. I would have nothing to do with it, so he wended his way back, ignoring all my immigrating colleagues and other gangplank embarkers. Why did this person pick me out, and indulge in this furious discussion to read my fortune? Would he have foretold that had I stayed I would have become something in the land I was leaving? He certainly did not, or was not able to, foretell that I would one day become a millionaire in New Zealand – (a joke!!) – who knows destiny?

In conclusion, I would like to record that despite all my protestations about being a relic of a lonely childhood and the subsequent effect on my life as a continuing loner, there was a phase in the saga where I knew deep friendship, comradeship, mateship, call it what one wishes. This was during my four years in the NZ Army and Air Force. Whether we were drawn too deeply to each other for the sake of self and mutual protection I do not know, but that sense of companionship is something I shall always treasure in remembrance. Also, I trust my children will remember the hunting/fishing trips and the many, many, many occasions we shared in our family life, endeavouring to bring them up in life – that was time for 'togetherness'.

Notes

1 A reference to the Ruamahanga River near Martinborough (NZ).

2 A variant of the Hindi *rani* meaning queen or princess; the female equivalent of raja.

APPENDIX TWO: ARRIVALS FROM KALIMPONG 1908–38

YEAR	PORT	NAME
1908	*Dunedin*	Williams, Leonard
		Williams, Sydney
1909	*Dunedin*	Boardman, Eustace
		Sinclair, Clarence
	Dunedin	Sinclair, Aileen
1910	*Dunedin*	Bishop, James
		Boardman, Eric
		Brooks, Tom
		Cruden, James
		May, Richard
1911	*Dunedin*	Mackay, Jean
		Mackay, John
		Hall, Harry
		Langmore, George
		Savigny, Patrick
1912	*Dunedin*	Cooper, Rose
		Fullerton, Evelyn
		Hall, William
		Higgins, Dorothy
		Hughes, Ernest
		Jones, Llewellyn
		O'Shannahan, Quinton
		Ochterlony, Mary
		Ochterlony, Robert
		Savigny, Helen
		Sinclair, Mae
		Snelleksz, Edward
		Stuart, Eric

YEAR	PORT	NAME
1914	*Dunedin*	Plaistowe, Gertrude
		Roberts, Molly
	Dunedin	Holder, Henry
		Lawless, Charles
		Lemare, Stuart
1915	*Dunedin*	Andrews, Adrian
		Bishop, Max
		Hall, Richard
		Melville, Hamilton
	Dunedin	Chambers, Molly
		Lawless, Minnie
		Sarkies, Kate
		Savigny, Minnie
		Pattison, Kate
		Pattison, Mary
1920	*Dunedin*	Brown, Annie
		Buckley, Terence
		Cullinan, Gordon
		Edbrooke, Kate
		King, Harry
		Snelleksz, Victor
		Sommerville, Hera
	Dunedin	Dinning, Margaret
		Graham, Esther
		Greig, Janet
		Greig, Mary
		Lyon, Robert
		Snelleksz, Wilfred

1915 group. *Mary Milne*

YEAR	PORT	NAME
1921	*Dunedin*	Chaston, Gwen
		Chaston, Mary
		Haslett, Mavis
		Moller, Dora
		Peters, George
		Peters, Lorna
1923	*Auckland*	Greig, Thomas
		Muspratt, Hugh
		Smith, Tom
1925	*Wellington*	Blackhall, Alexander
		Gammie, Elizabeth
		Gammie, Fergus
		O'Brien, Peggy
		Watson, Charles
		Watson, Thomas
	Wellington	Bayley, Clarence
		Brooks, Horace
		Dinning, Annie
		Duncan, Miriam
		Gammie, Moira
		Gollan, Amy
		Greig, Helen
		Hawkins, Richard
		Keelan, Thomas
		Penny, John
		Reid, James
		Robertson, George
		Royston, Eva
		Spalding, Charles
		Speed, Thomas
		Spencer, Roland
		Stevenson, Michael
1926	*Wellington*	Allcard, Alice
		Allcard, Violet
		Fox, Margaret
		Gammie, Alison
		MacIntyre, Donald
		Macey, Richard
		Mason, Eva
		Mortimore, Jane
		Mortimore, Rend
		Moss-Hayes, Oscar
		Peters, Alice
		Smith, Alice
		Smith, Margaret
		Spalding, Thomas
		Stuart, Alison
		Walker, Constance
		White, George
1928	*Wellington*	French, Deborah
		Howie, Mary
		Moller, Charles
		Scott, Anne
		Speed, Constance
		Tweedie, Lucy
1929	*Wellington*	Boden, Lucy
		Davenport, Ellie
		Kennedy, Jessie
		Moller, Elizabeth
		Spaul, Elsa

YEAR	PORT	NAME
1938	*Wellington*	Anderson, Peter
		Bayley, Colin
		Beaton, William
		Berkeley, Dorothy
		Gammie, Gavin
		Gammie, Kathleen
		Kennedy, Thornton
		Leith, Fred
		Lethaby, Pamela
		McKenzie, John
		Nicholls, Sheila
		Radcliffe, Beryl
		Tweedie, Hamish
		Stuart, Reginald

The SS Janus, *1925*

ACKNOWLEDGEMENTS

This book has been taking shape since I first made contact with a Kalimpong descendant (the wonderful Pam Gardiner) in 2011. From the outset, descendants have been generous in sharing photographs and documents from private family collections. I thank you all. I am particularly grateful for the efforts of those whose collections make up a substantial portion of this book: Judi Cassidy, Anne Beckett, Jim Gammie, the Langmore family, Mary Milne and her daughter Carol Ridgway, Sylvia Slater and of course my dad, for his timely sharing of Lorna's photos. Anne, Mary and Sylvia were all fountains of knowledge about the Wellington community and further south: their input was essential to bring detail to many of the images. I know inevitably there will be mistakes, and I take full responsibility for those. We all hope that committing these details to print will prevent further loss of knowledge about the New Zealand Kalimpong community. I also want to acknowledge the trust that each family has placed in me to position their particular story – each of which is extraordinary in its own right – within the collective narrative of this community. It has been a privilege to do so. Special thanks to the Beaton family for allowing me to reproduce excerpts from Bill Beaton's precious memoir.

In 2016 I was awarded a New Zealand History Research Trust Award for this project by the Ministry of Culture and Heritage. I am grateful for the window of dedicated time and travel that this funding enabled. The book was a part-time project through several years of teaching in the Department of History and Art History at the University of Otago, and I benefitted from ongoing conversations with colleagues about it. Ngaire Gardner, who has her own extraordinary family connection to British India, offered much appreciated visual expertise; and Tiffany Cone, who was there at the beginning, came in with magical feedback at the end. Otago University Press has been supportive through the various stages of bringing this book together. So too have my family, and my partner Luke Smythe, whose meticulous eye for visual detail and textual precision I can only aspire to emulate! Thanks also to Luke's parents, Claire and Stephen, at whose light place in Matakana over a couple of intensive weeks in 2018 I selected and arranged the Kalimpong photographs into the visual narrative presented here. Final thanks must go to Fiona Moffat, designer at Otago University Press, whose fabulous design has made this story shine.

REFERENCES

Kalimpong Papers, National Library of Scotland, Edinburgh

McCabe, Jane, *Race, Tea and Colonial Resettlement: Imperial families, interrupted*, New York, London: Bloomsbury Academic, 2017

McCabe, Jane, 'Kalimpong Kids: The lives and labours of Anglo-Indian adolescents resettled in New Zealand, 1908–1938', PhD diss., University of Otago, 2014

Minto, James, *Graham of Kalimpong*, Edinburgh: Blackwood, 1974

Nicholls, Frank, *Assam Shikari: A tea planter's story of hunting and high adventure in the jungles of North East India,* New Zealand: Tonson Publishing House, 1970

Mainwaring, Simon, *A Century of Children,* Kalimpong: Dr Graham's Homes, 2000

St Andrew's Colonial Homes Magazine, National Library of Scotland, Edinburgh

Suggested Reading

Barker, George, *A Tea Planter's Life in Assam*, Calcutta: Thacker, Spink & Co, 1884

Caplan, Lionel, *Children of Colonialism: Anglo-Indians in a postcolonial world*, Oxford: Berg, 2001

McFarlane, Iris, *Daughters of the Empire*, New Delhi: Oxford University Press, 2006

McQueen, Alison, *The Secret Children*, London: Orion Books, 2012

McMenamin, Dorothy, *Raj Days to Downunder*, Christchurch: Dorothy McMenamin, 2010

Online Resources

www.kalimpongkids.org.nz
www.koi-hai.com
www.fibis.org
www.drgrahamshomes.net

INDEX

Bold denotes illustrations and tables.